A
REVOLUTION
IN A
DECADE.

ten out of ten

D0587454

Alan Boyle and Salli Humphreys

First published 2012
By Leannta Publishing
63 Arlington Avenue, London N1 7BA

A catalogue record for this book is available from the
British Library.

ISBN 978-0-9563760-3-9

Designed by the in-house design team,
The Learning Trust, Hackney, London

Printed and bound in the UK by City Printing

Dedication

To the children of Hackney and their teachers. May they always learn from each others' exceptional talents.

Contents

Acknowledgements

1 **Introduction** 1

2 **Setting the scene** 7

3 **Raising Standards** 15

4 **Closing the gap** 19

5 **10cc** 23

   Concept 30

   Capacity 53

   Challenge 66

   Courage 76

   Creativity 84

   Collaboration 93

   Confidence 102

   Communication 112

   Celebration 117

   Consistency 121

6 **Conclusion** 127

7 **Milestones** 131

8 **Conversations** 135

   References 137

   Index 141

Acknowledgements

We would like to thank all those in The Learning Trust and beyond who gave of their valuable time and allowed us to interview them and use their words to help us piece together what the Learning Trust did to enable it to move education forward in the way it has.

A very **big** thank you goes especially to: Gabriella Beckles – Raymond and Sandy Barnes for their help in organising the meetings.

Finally we must thank the board of The Learning Trust for allowing us to infiltrate and find out exactly how it was done.

We enjoyed it.

After all:

Knowledge is in the end based on acknowledgement.

Ludwig Wittgenstein

1 Introduction

In November 2000 Hackney was in chaos. The council, once ruled by Herbert Morrison, was bankrupt and faced a potential £40million deficit.[1] All spending, including that in schools, was frozen. What had gone wrong? The answer to which is 'Just about everything.' The council's own advertisement to recruit a chief executive in 1999 said the person appointed would face 'an absence of coherent political leadership, a disconnection between strategy and operation, poor financial management and a lack of focus on basic services.' Whoever applied couldn't say they hadn't been warned.

The Government had also been warned. In a statement to Parliament in 1997, the local MP Brian Sedgemore blew the whistle and urged the Government to intervene for the sake of Hackney schoolchildren. In his request to the House of Commons he describes Tony Elliston, the chief executive of Hackney Council until 1999, as a 'public school bully masquerading as an East End barrow boy'. Sedgemore goes on to say: 'You probably will not believe this, Mr. Deputy Speaker, but last week I was browsing in the Library through a magazine called "PR Week", of which I have a copy with me. Speaking of what he described as "maverick teachers" in Hackney, Tony Elliston, at a meeting of the Institute of Public Relations, said: "Hackney is always in the shit. It's just a question of how deep it is". Speaking, furthermore, about Ms Lorraine Langham, an executive director of the council, he said: "Lorraine's approach to the media is that you can't polish a turd."'[2] Elliston continued as chief executive for two more years despite announcing on a national radio programme in 1997 that

[1] Audit Commission, November 2000: 'Hackney LBC Corporate Governance inspection'

[2] Hansard 1 December 1997: columns 130–132

he was ready to go to war with the Government over Hackney's education services.

While that may be shocking, what is more appalling is that five years later, in 2002, after three LEA Ofsted inspections, intervention by the Hackney Improvement Team and partial privatisation of education services, Hackney was still firmly rooted at the bottom of the school league tables. No surprise that parents were struggling to move their children to secondary schools in other boroughs.

Fast forward to 2012 and the situation has been reversed. Hackney parents are struggling to get their children into Hackney secondary schools along with parents who live outside the borough. Hackney's primary and secondary school results are now above the national averages. The changes that have taken place since 2002 are dramatic and astonishing. Education in Hackney has been completely transformed; it is a revolution within a decade. The question 'How did that happen?' was the stimulus for our research.

Sir Michael Barber, who was the first chair of the education committee on Hackney council in 1990 and later went on to head the Prime Minister Blair's delivery unit from 2001–2005, wrote a chapter in 'Change Wars' where he compared research into system improvement to that of school improvement.[3] In the 1980s the leading research in education was around school effectiveness. By the mid 1990s, we could describe an effective school but that didn't tell us much about how to create one so the research focus shifted to school improvement. Barber argues that research about education systems rather than schools has now reached the same point. He claims that research has enabled us to describe an effective school system and the time has come to look at how to improve school systems. Barber

[3] Barber, M. (2009) *From System Effectiveness to System Improvement: Reform Paradigms and Relationships.*

In Hargreaves, A. & Fullan, M. Change Wars. Bloomington: Solution Tree

questions 'What kind of reforms and what approaches to implementation will be most successful in enabling systems to achieve effectiveness?' A good question and one we attempt to respond to through this research.

In 2007 McKinsey and Company examined 25 school systems around the world, including ten of the top performers.[4] This was a good foundation that enabled them to describe the common attributes across these generally acknowledged effective education systems. It was followed by a second report in 2010 which looked at 20 effective school systems to determine how these effective systems continued to improve.[5] In this second report McKinsey studied a very diverse range of systems: large and small, centralised and de-centralised, public and private across five continents with a wide array of performance levels. It essentially provides insights into how to sustain improvements in systems that are already working well.

We know from research into failing schools that the improvement processes which work in normal schools will not work in a school with serious weaknesses.[6] If education systems behave like schools then we would not be surprised to find that strategies to sustain improvements in systems that are already effective might not be appropriate for failing education systems. In 'Performance Beyond Expectations', Hargreaves et al report about two education systems, Tower Hamlets and Walsall, that made significant improvements from a very low base.[7] In Walsall's case things were so bad that the services were removed from the council and privatised. Our research in Hackney complements and extends this knowledge. Conditions in Hackney in 2002 were far worse that either Tower Hamlets or Walsall at their low points.

The research was funded by Leannta Education Associates, a private company that promotes high

4 McKinsey & Co. (2007) How the World's best-performing school systems come out on top. The report is available online at: www.mckinsey.com/clientservice/social_sector/our_practices/education/knowledge_highlights/best_performing_school.aspx

5 McKinsey & Co. (2010) How the World's most improved school systems keep getting better. The report is available online at: www.mckinsey.com/clientservice/Social_Sector/our_practices/Education/Knowledge_Highlights/How%20School%20Systems%20Get%20Better.aspx

6 Boyle, A. (2007) Compassionate Intervention in Blankstein, Cole & Houston. Engaging Every Learner. Thousand Oaks: Corwin

7 Hargreaves, A. et al (2011) Performance beyond expectations. National College for School Leadership. The report is available online at: www.nationalcollege.org.uk/performance-beyond-expectations

quality professional learning in education. Alan Boyle from Leannta was involved in the 'Performance Beyond Expectation' study with Professors Andy Hargreaves and Alma Harris for the National College for School Leadership and the Specialist Schools and Academies Trust and wrote the case story about system-wide improvements in Tower Hamlets, the neighbouring borough to Hackney[8]. Salli Humphreys is an outstanding teacher and freelance education consultant who was Learning Director for Leannta Education Associates during this research.

This study is an in-depth analysis of how the worst school system in England improved to become outstanding in ten years. We know what happened – the education service for Hackney was removed from the council and contracted to a private not-for-profit company called The Learning Trust. But that does not answer the question 'How?' From our research we found ten characteristics that when combined explain how The Learning Trust revolutionised education in Hackney during the course of its ten-year contract; ten out of ten.

We interviewed a wide cross-section of people who were involved with Hackney education over the life of The Learning Trust's contract, ranging from the Secretary of State for Education at the time the contract was awarded to front line staff in The Learning Trust. We found people who described themselves as 'relics' of the Inner London Education Authority (ILEA) who had lived and worked in Hackney even before schools were transferred to the council in 1990. Many of the people we listened to live in Hackney and sent their children to Hackney schools. Overall, we recorded conversations with 36 people which, in total, lasted in excess of 25 hours.

Our conversations followed a loose structure where we asked people to respond to four broad questions:

1. Who are you and what is your involvement with Hackney education?

2. Why do you think Hackney's GCSE and national test scores have improved so much since 2002?

3. What contributions (if any) did The Learning Trust make to these improvements?

4. Is there anything else you would like to add that you think would help our investigation?

We used an appreciative inquiry approach to the study by steering our conversations to things that had been successful and made a positive difference. We avoided dwelling on the problems that existed in Hackney before 2002 by focusing on the solutions to those problems. We made audio recording of all our conversations. The conversations were coded and analysed. We then applied a triangulation technique to determine the key issues from the coded conversations. We decided that if at least three people expressed a common view from completely different perspectives then we considered that to be a reliable insight. By perspectives, we mean opinions from people with completely different roles. For example, we did not count statements made by three different headteachers as coming from different perspectives. Although they were made separately, by different people, the views came from the same perspective, that of a headteacher. From our analysis we found a genuine consensus around ten characteristics. Each of them is supported by at least three different perspectives and most were agreed by five or six. We consider each characteristic to be highly reliable. By coincidence we could label each characteristic with a word beginning with the letter 'C'. We use alliteration for the 10 'C' characteristics, or 10cc, to make them more memorable.

Our title is drawn from our conversation with Estelle Morris who described what The Learning Trust has achieved as 'a revolution in a decade', combined with the outcomes of our analysis – ten characteristics from the ten year contract.

We hope you enjoy reading about the good news from Hackney. It has been a privilege to be able to complete this research.

2 Setting the scene

Hackney, one of the 12 inner London boroughs, was formed in 1965 when the former borough of Hackney was amalgamated with Stoke Newington to the north west and Shoreditch in the south west corner, adjacent to the City of London. Its southern border is shared with Bethnal Green and Bow which is now part of Tower Hamlets. Hackney merges inconspicuously with Islington to the west and Haringey to the north while its eastern boundary is formed by the lower reaches of the river Lea and Hackney marshes which create the natural open spaces between Hackney and Waltham Forest. Hackney covers a geographical area of 19 square km (7.4 sq. miles).

1. Hammersmith &Fulham
2. Kensington & Chelsea
3. Westminster
4. Islington
5. Southwark
6. City

About 220,000 people live in Hackney. It is ethnically diverse and it is estimated that over 100 languages are spoken by residents. Of the resident population, 40% describe themselves as White British and 15% are in other White ethnic groups; 30% are Black or Black British; 9.4% are Asian or Asian British; 4% describe themselves as 'Mixed', and 3% as Chinese or Other.[9] The Hackney Household Survey in 2004 found that 66% of residents spoke only English at home; 22% claimed it was the main language they used and 12% said they did not speak English at home. In 2004 Hackney was rated as the most deprived borough in England.[10] In the 2010 survey it was still the most deprived part of London and the sixth most deprived in England. Clearly, between 2002–2012 there were high levels of poverty across the borough. We know from research in education that there is a high correlation between poverty and low educational outcomes.[11]

From 1965 the Inner London Education Authority (ILEA) was responsible for all schools in Hackney and the other inner London boroughs until it was abolished in 1990. Apart from the growth of children's centres since 2000, the number of schools in Hackney has remained roughly the same since the ILEA days although some schools closed and were replaced by others. There are currently: 55 primary or nursery schools, 23 children's centres, seven secondary schools, five academies, four special schools and two pupil referral units in Hackney.[12] When Hackney took over responsibility for education in 1990, GCSE results among the 10 secondary schools within the borough were among the lowest in the country. In 1990 only 14% of students gained 5 or more GCSE grades A–C, compared with a national average of 34.5%.[13]

All the inner London local education authorities (LEAs) started from scratch in 1990 and had to establish new organisations to support schools at a time when

[9] UK census, 2001

[10] Indices of deprivation are compiled by the Communities and Local Government Department and are available online at www.imd.communities. gov.uk

[11] Raffo et al (2007), 'A review of research on the links between education and poverty.' York: Joseph Rowntree Foundation

[12] Academies are independent secondary schools funded directly by the Government.

[13] Department for Education Freedom of Information request 2011

schools and LEAs all over England were implementing the national curriculum and local management of schools.[14] It was a significant challenge. Hackney, Islington, Tower Hamlets, Lambeth and Southwark were all closely monitored by Government officials as schools in these boroughs had the lowest GCSE results (and after 1996, key stage 2 results) in England. Her Majesty's Inspectors (HMI) inspected all secondary schools and three quarters of primary schools within the borough as they were transferred from the ILEA to Hackney. They reported their findings to the Secretary of State for education and the fledgling LEA.[15]

The HMI report is shocking. In primary schools, 42% of 400 lessons observed in Hackney were unsatisfactory, compared with 30% nationally at the time. Schools overall were judged between adequate and poor. Six were causing serious concern; in other words they were failing schools. In secondary schools over 40% of lessons observed were unsatisfactory or worse but the findings were uneven. 'A striking feature of the secondary schools is the marked disparity between them. In four, although none was outstanding, the quality of the work came close to the national average with around two-thirds of all lessons reaching an acceptable standard. In the Hackney context, that is no mean achievement. In the other four, between half and three-quarters of all lessons were less than satisfactory.'[16]

Hackney's first Director of Education, Gus John, responded to the 1990 HMI report by establishing the Hackney Action Research Project (HARP). He presented a report about HARP outcomes to Hackney education committee in 1991. The report reveals that HARP's main activities were linked to management of primary schools.[17] It is apparent that many primary school headteachers in the borough were struggling with their newly delegated responsibilities under the local

[14] The Education Reform Act 1988 introduced the first national curriculum in England and forced local authorities to delegate at least 80% of all education funding to schools to be managed locally by each individual school governing body. These were massive changes for schools at the time.

[15] Schools in Hackney: Some Issues. A report by HMI 1990. Published by Department for Education & Science. Ref: 200/90/DS

[16] Ibid

[17] Minutes of Hackney Education Committee Meeting, 10.12.91

management of schools initiative (LMS). The report indicates the urgent need for management support and leadership development in Hackney primary schools. We found no evidence that any subsequent support had a wide impact on these schools.

The period from 1994–1996 was politically turbulent in Hackney and two education stories hit the headlines in the national press: the closure of Hackney Downs secondary school and the 'Romeo and Juliet' affair at Kingsmead Primary school. Hackney Downs failed an Ofsted inspection in 1994. Gus John advised the Council to close the school because it had declined too far.[18] The school was once outstanding and its alumni include: Harold Pinter, Steven Berkoff, Michael Caine and Lord Goodman. But after years of decay it became a hopeless case, without the capacity to improve itself. Closure was opposed strenuously by left-wing activists in the local Labour party.

At Kingsmead Primary, the headteacher refused to accept free tickets for pupils to attend a Romeo & Juliet ballet because it was 'a blatantly heterosexual love story'. The tabloid press were tipped off and it became front page news in all the popular national newspapers.[19] Gus John advised the governors to suspend the headteacher and conduct an investigation into gross misconduct. This incited gay activists and opposition to Gus John started spreading. The Kingsmead governors refused to follow the Director's advice and in July 1995 Hackney Council tried to overturn the decision to close Hackney Downs. Despite this, Hackney Downs closed in December that year. By this time the left-wing faction of the Labour group had gained control of Hackney Council. Gus John resigned in 1996, accused councillors of behaving like gangsters and took his case to three industrial tribunals.[20] Meanwhile, GCSE results in Hackney were slowly improving.

[18] Michael Barber provides an illuminating account of the closure of Hackney Downs in Barber, M. (1996) 'The Learning Game'. London: Victor Gollancz

[19] 'Teacher in 'Romeo & Juliet' row apologises', Will Brown, The Independent, 21 January 1994.

[20] 'Labour set to bar the party within'. Mark Whitehead, Times Educational Supplement, 9 August 1996

This high-profile media attention gave Hackney the label of 'looney-left'. In 1997 David Blunkett, the first Secretary of State for education in the newly elected Blair government, sent Ofsted into Hackney to report on the LEA.[21] Ofsted was fiercely critical and reported that Hackney LEA was failing to meet some of its statutory responsibilities. Stephen Byers, the minister for schools at the time, declared Hackney as 'the worst LEA in the country' and it was apparent that political knives were out for Hackney's throat.[22] By this time the council was in political turmoil and was effectively powerless. There was still no director of education; all the second tier education officers had left and the administration was weak. The Government forced the council to bring the Hackney Improvement Team (HIT) into the borough. They were immediately referred to as the 'HIT squad'. Meanwhile Blunkett started legislation that would give the Secretary of State the power to intervene in failing LEAs. Despite this furore, Haggerston and Clapton schools were among the top 10 secondary schools across England in terms of their value-added GCSE results.

In January 1998 Liz Reid was appointed as Director of Education and the 'HIT squad' published an interim report revealing a shortfall of £3m in the education budget. The final report in July noted some slight improvement but there were still areas of concern.[23] Before the end of the year the Government had passed the new law giving it powers to take over failing LEAs and in January 1999 Blunkett invited tenders from private companies to intervene in LEAs. A list of approved private contractors was prepared. After another critical Ofsted report in March 1999, Blunkett announced that Hackney would be the first LEA to have some of its powers removed.[24] A three-year contract was agreed with Nord Anglia to run Hackney's School Improvement Service and the Ethnic Minority Service

[21] Office for Standards in Education (Ofsted) is responsible for inspecting all schools and local authorities in England. Inspection reports are publically available on the website: www.ofsted. gov.uk

[22] 'Borough of hate and hit squads.' David Walker & Rebecca Smithers, The Guardian, 19 March 1999

[23] 'Hackney still failing to support its schools.' BBC News, 21 July 1998, http://news. bbc.co.uk/1/hi/ education/136830.stm

[24] 'Hackney's troubled past.' BBC News, 19 March 1999, http:// news.bbc.co.uk/1/hi/ education/299656.stm

from September 1999. The remainder of the LEA functions were retained by the council. In the following year, 2000, the Audit Commission reported that the whole council was virtually bankrupt with a shortfall of £21m in its budget.[25] Only half the council tax had been collected for years on end and one Hackney councillor told the press: "Our fingers are not on the pulse of the borough, but on each others' throats." Another said that simply to arrange a meeting was like "wading through treacle laced with razor blades."[26] No one denied that Hackney had mountainous problems. When Hackney primary schools came bottom of the London league tables it probably had something to do with the levels of deprivation, but also with being in a 'basket-case' LEA. Liz Reid, the well-regarded director of the now partly privatised education service, resigned after only two and a half years in the job. Hackney Council was declared a killer, 'the Bates motel of local government.'[27] And in November 2000, the third Ofsted inspection report eventually reached a conclusion that had been painfully obvious to many people for several years: '*We do not believe that Hackney LEA has the capacity to provide a secure, stable context for continuous educational improvement. The time has come for radical change.*'[28]

Radical change came in the formation of The Learning Trust, the first not-for-profit private company to run education services for an entire borough. This was a preferred solution to the profit-making privatisation in neighbouring Islington because the Government recognised that Hackney Council did not have sufficient capacity to manage such a private contract.[29] The decision may also have been influenced by reports in the media about profits made by Nord Anglia, under the partial privatisation, at the expense of the poorest community in England.[30] As a political solution it appealed to the right, who declared that it would rescue

[25] Audit Commission, November 2000: 'Hackney LBC Corporate Governance inspection'

[26] '*Hackney Council a load of rubbish*.' Paul Barker, London Evening Standard, 9 November 2000

[27] Ibid

[28] Ofsted (2000). Inspection of Hackney Local Education Authority.

[29] '*Hackney Council stripped of right to run schools*.' Sarah Cassidy, Independent on Sunday, 18 October 2001

[30] '*Nord Anglia to run Hackney school services*.' BBC News, 18 June 1999, http://news.bbc.co.uk/1/hi/education/372575.stm

the education of some of the most deprived children in England from the malign influence of Hackney Council. And to the left who claimed it was a death blow to the profit-making privatisation of education services.

Alan Wood was appointed Director of Education by Hackney Council in 2001. He was previously Director in Lambeth, another challenging inner London LEA, and he arrived with a successful track record. His first priority was to manage the transfer of education services from the council to The Learning Trust where he became the chief executive and provided the stable leadership that was desperately needed at the time. Alan continued to lead The Learning Trust throughout its existence.

The Learning Trust took over in September 2002 with a 10 year contract. Sir Mike Tomlinson, Her Majesty's Chief Inspector at Ofsted until April 2002, became the first chairman of The Learning Trust. A year later, 2003, Ofsted were back, together with the Audit Commission, to inspect services under The Learning Trust. This time they reported rapid progress overall. Even though many services were still unsatisfactory or even poor, Ofsted noted improvements in 18 services. It was a good start by The Learning Trust but although some good news was welcome, standards remained the lowest in England. GCSE and national test scores were all well below the national average in 2003. Although GCSE results had improved from 1998–2003, it was at a lower rate than the national trend. National test results for eleven year-olds in Hackney actually fell in 2003, while they continued to improve nationally.

[31] General Certificate of Secondary Education (GCSE) examinations are usually taken by students aged 16 in different subjects. They mark the end of compulsory education in England. Grades, ranging from A*–G are awarded according to performance in each subject. Until 2004, the national benchmark was to achieve grade C or higher in at least five different subjects. School and local authority performance tables are based on the percentage of students who achieved five or more GCSE grades A*–C. The benchmark was modified to include English and mathematics as compulsory subjects after 2004. These data are available from the school and college performance tables. www.education.gov.uk/performancetables

3 Raising standards

Charts 1–4 show GCSE results (for 16 year-olds) in Hackney from 1990, when schools were transferred from the ILEA. In 2004, the Government changed the national comparison to include English and mathematics within the five GCSE grades. We have included a common year, 2004, on both measures for comparative purposes.[31]

Chart 1 Percentage of students with 5+ GCSE grades A*–C in England and Hackney.

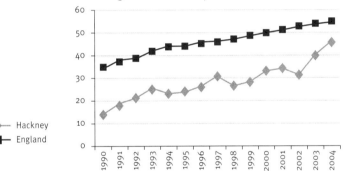

Hackney
England

Closing the Gap

Chart 2 Gap between percentage of students in Hackney gaining 5+ GCSE grades A*–C and the national average.

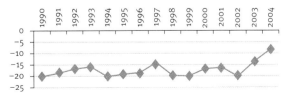

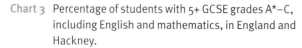

Chart 3   Percentage of students with 5+ GCSE grades A*–C,
including English and mathematics, in England and
Hackney.

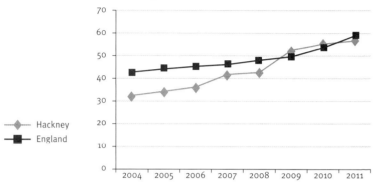

Closing the Gap

Chart 4   Gap between percentage of students in Hackney
gaining 5+ GCSE grades A*–C, including English and
mathematics, and the national average.

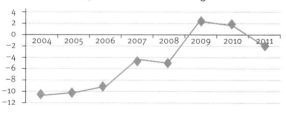

Charts 5–8 show national test scores (for 11 year-olds)
at end of key stage 2 from 1996, the first year that
results were published.[32] Chart 5 shows the aggregate
percentage of students reaching the expected level
(level 4) or higher in English, mathematics and science.
The science national test was discontinued after 2009.
The Government benchmark is now the percentage of
students who achieve level 4 or higher in both English
and mathematics. Charts 7 and 8 compare Hackney
with the national average since 2006 using this new
benchmark.

[32] National tests are taken
by all primary students
at age 11 and marked
externally. These data
are also available in
the school and college
performance tables.
www.education.gov.uk/
performancetables

Chart 5   Aggregate percentage of students achieving level 4+ in English, mathematics and science national tests at end of key stage 2 for England and Hackney.

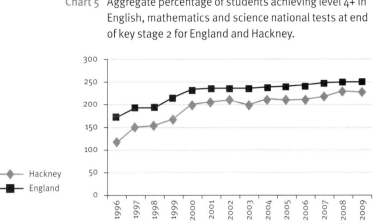

Closing the Gap

Chart 6   Gap between aggregate percentage of students in Hackney achieving level 4+ in English, mathematics and science national tests at end of key stage 2 and the national average.

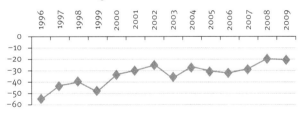

% level 4 in English and maths age 11

Chart 7   Percentage of students who achieve level 4 or higher in national tests for both English and mathematics at end of key stage 2 for England and Hackney.

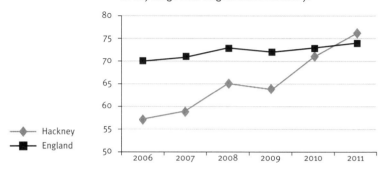

Closing the Gap

Chart 8   Gap between the percentage of students from Hackney achieving level 4 or higher in national tests for both English and mathematics at end of key stage 2 and national average.

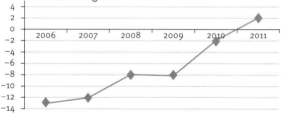

These are impressive improvements in educational outcomes since 2002. We have already noted that the relationship between multiple deprivation and achievement in education is extensively researched and well documented. What makes these results so startling is the fact that the latest national statistics (2011) show that Hackney is still the most deprived borough in London and the sixth most deprived in England.[33]

[33] Communities and Local Government: The English Indices of Deprivation 2010. Published 24 March 2011.

4 Closing the gap

GCSE results and national test scores from 2002–2011 show the improvements across Hackney schools over the length of The Learning Trust's contract. These data reveal a remarkable recovery and evidence of steady and sustained improvement in Hackney education. The gaps between Hackney and the national averages were not only closed, they were opened on the positive side. Primary and secondary school performances in Hackney are now better than the national averages. With students at two more academies yet to reach Year 11 and contribute their grades to the Hackney average, the prospects for continued growth and even higher performance are good.

The improvements over a relatively short time period represent a complete transformation of education in Hackney; a revolution in a decade. Our research focus was clear:

- How did The Learning Trust achieve these system-wide improvements?

We have outlined our research methodology in the introduction. Through detailed and focused conversations with a wide range of people who were involved with Hackney education over the length of The Learning Trust's contract, we were able to gather views from diverse perspectives to support our investigation. Our analysis of the coded conversations revealed a clear consensus of views about the reasons for the success achieved by The Learning Trust. We present this informed consensus as ten characteristics of The Learning Trust, each beginning with the letter 'C':

- Concept
- Capacity
- Challenge
- Courage
- Creativity
- Collaboration
- Confidence
- Communication
- Celebration
- Consistency

This is not meant to be a check list or a blueprint for other system-wide improvements. These characteristics are inter-dependent and it is the combination of these ten touchstones that made the difference. We explain what we mean by each individual characteristic below, but first we present a visual model that shows how the ten characteristics coalesce.

Capacity building is the core of systemic improvement; we know this from the organisations studied by McKinsey and from Michael Fullan's work.[34] Our analysis shows that capacity is supported by four separate characteristics: challenge, courage, creativity and collaboration. Each of these makes an important individual contribution to the systemic improvements so we have reported on them individually but together they create synergy that adds more to capacity.

Confidence was an important feature in the transformation. As with capacity, we found other characteristics that were powerful enough in their own right to be identified individually. Acting together, communication and celebration built confidence to a higher level.

[34] Fullan, M. (2010) All Systems Go. Thousand Oaks: Corwin

Above all we describe the concept behind The Learning Trust as the most significant feature. It is remarkable that a relatively young organisation can establish such a powerful identity; it is a tribute to the resolute leadership evident at all levels in the organisation. Resolute leadership relies on consistency and this, combined with the concept, is what matters most.

10CC
Ten characteristics of The Learning Trust that transformed education in Hackney

Capacity	Confidence	Concept
● Challenge	● Communication	● Consistency
● Courage	● Celebration	
● Creativity		
● Collaboration		

5 **10CC**

To begin with we describe each of the ten characteristics. Then we explore each one individually by presenting evidence to explain how The Learning Trust displays this feature in its work.

Concept

The Learning Trust is a unique organisation; we found no other account of a private not-for-profit company administering schools for an entire borough. Just being different from the previous failed administration did not make The Learning Trust successful; it required much more than that. Over the ten years of its contract, The Learning Trust established a powerful identity that encompasses its values, beliefs and way of working. It set a clear vision from the outset that all students in Hackney could do as well as students anywhere else. The ambition, which it achieved, was that after ten years parents would struggle to get their children into a Hackney school. The Learning Trust 'brand' is now a collective identity which is widely shared. This is the driving force behind the transformation in Hackney's education. It goes way beyond mission statements, compelling visions and inspirational dreams because it is based on action and reality. We use the word 'concept' to describe what The Learning Trust has established that makes it so successful and we illustrate the concept by referring to how it developed and works.

Capacity

Improving the leadership and skills within any organisation is the obvious way to improve its performance. We refer to this as capacity building and although it could hardly be considered a secret, it is one of Michael Fullan's six secrets of change.[35] Recruiting the best people and investing in their continued professional development are intuitively the right things to do and this is how The Learning Trust set about building capacity. We learn about how they overcame difficulties at the beginning caused by many key vacancies and people reluctant to come to Hackney. Our study reveals how The Learning Trust head-hunted people; utilised existing capacity already in place; developed new leadership programmes and looked outwards to grow intellectual capacity. Capacity building is the heart of The Learning Trust's work; this is how education in Hackney was transformed.

Our analysis indicates how capacity was increased by four separate characteristics acting in combination: challenge, courage, creativity & collaboration. Each of these is powerful in its own right which is why we report on each one separately. The important outcome from this research is how it reveals the synergy between these four characteristics and how the combination contributes to capacity building.

Challenge

Pressure and support are the yin and yang of capacity building in schools.[36] In the previous section we explore how The Learning Trust provided support through capacity building. Here, we learn how The Learning Trust exerted pressure by challenging the community, school leaders, teachers and its own staff. There are no cosy relationships or comfort zones in The Learning Trust. While it provides the best possible support, it has the highest expectations of everyone's performance in return. We learn how a no-nonsense approach to under-performing schools ensured that Hackney became the most improved borough in

[35] Fullan, M. (2008), Six Secrets of Change. San Francisco: Jossey Bass

[36] David Maclean describes a systematic approach used to provide challenge and support to schools in Woods, D. & Cribb, M. (2001) Effective LEAs and School Improvement. London: Routledge Falmer

England, in terms of education, during The Learning Trust's contract. Our study indicates that a symbiotic relationship between challenge and support is at the core of capacity-building which, in turn, drives systemic improvement.

Courage

Courage is a character trait that compels us to take actions that we know will lead us into danger. It is not about being fearless; it takes courage to overcome fear and deal with the predictable unpleasant consequences. Some people consider that The Learning Trust displayed courage just by taking over education in Hackney at a time when standards were rock bottom and the council was chaotic. However, leaders in The Learning Trust would disagree. They consider that there was nothing to fear from the contract to run the education services in Hackney. Instead it was a huge opportunity to make system-wide improvements.

With hindsight, we would agree with this. However, it is beyond dispute that some of the actions taken by people in The Learning Trust, to bring about rapid systemic improvement, were very courageous. Consequently it is one of our ten touchstones. We learn about the courage needed to speak the truth and face reality, to get to grips with failure in school leadership, to close schools in the face of strong opposition, to embrace the politically unpopular academies programme and to take risks.

Creativity

When The Learning Trust was created in 2002, it was an entirely new concept. A not-for-profit private company running a public education service was innovative and certainly something for the 21st Century. It would have been odd for this new organisation to look back to the 20th century and base the way in which it would operate on the pre-existing methods and systems used by Hackney Council. Consequently, it seems almost natural that The Learning Trust would do things differently and it is no surprise to find that creativity is one of its defining characteristics. In describing The Fourth Way as a way forward after the failures of earlier reform efforts, Hargreaves and Shirley identify learning that is creative, engaging and demanding as one of its characteristics.[37] Here we find The Learning Trust was always ready to innovate and take risks. Released from council bureaucracy enabled The Learning Trust to act swiftly and with agility. Executive action encouraged managers to take responsibility. People were empowered to do what they thought was best and knew they would not be blamed for taking risks. Under these conditions we find that creativity flourishes and this made a significant contribution to capacity-building in Hackney.

Collaboration

Collaboration essentially means working together in order to achieve a shared goal. The benefits are obvious, when people from different organisations collaborate then capacity increases and the chances of achieving the desired outcome are improved. In terms of capacity building, there are potentially huge gains without much additional investment. The key is to find and prioritise the common good or moral purpose that would motivate a collective effort. For The Learning Trust the moral purpose was very clear – raising educational standards of all students in Hackney.

We learn how The Learning Trust successfully created collaboration between Government, who had the money, sponsors who had altruistic motives and Hackney Council who owned the land, to build five brand new academies for the benefit of students in

[37] Hargreaves, A. & Shirley, D. (2009), The Fourth Way: The inspiring future for educational change. Thousand Oaks: Corwin

Hackney. The speed and political dimensions of this make it an amazing achievement.

Individual schools are naturally more concerned about the performance of their own students than those in other schools. We also explore how The Learning Trust developed strong collaboration between primary schools in Hackney to the extent that highly successful schools were willing to federate and share their expertise with failing schools. The primary school federations in Hackney have transformed failing schools into outstanding ones in record times.

While collaboration is a powerful feature of the systemic improvements in Hackney, it is accompanied by a competitive edge that plays an important part in raising the bar even higher.

Confidence

Confidence is the foundation of any organisation's success; it often separates winners from losers. We learn how confidence connects the high expectations of The Learning Trust to its performance and that of the schools in Hackney. Rosbeth Moss Kanter enlightens us by describing how sports, business and education organisations turn a downward spiral into a winning streak by growing confidence.[38] The story of The Learning Trust complements the cases that she uncovered.

Our study reveals the fundamental importance that leadership of The Learning Trust played to inspire confidence in order to attract the extraordinary investments of time, effort and resources that were necessary to transform education in Hackney in such a short time. Inspirational leadership quickly motivated people within The Learning Trust, in Hackney schools and in the wider community. Ferocious assertion that failure is unacceptable soon raised aspirations.

[38]Kanter, R. M. (2004) Confidence. London: Random House

Mid-term the mantra changed to all schools will be good or better. Students and staff are justifiably proud to be in Hackney. Our analysis shows that confidence was boosted by the next two characteristics which are tightly inter-linked: communication and celebration. Because each of these dimensions is important in its own right, we describe them separately.

Communication

Trust relies on good communication that is frequent, open and honest. In their book about Sustainable Leadership, Hargreaves and Fink describe the importance of communication trust.[39] What we find from The Learning Trust is that success in communication is not about how clear your vision is, or how much charisma you have, or how slick your powerpoints are. It's about how well you listen. The art of communication is knowing whether your message has been received as you intended. The Learning Trust was good at listening and then taking appropriate action. We learn how excellent communications in all aspects helped to build trust and boost confidence. Within the organisation people feel valued as they are listened to. Leaders talk to everyone on the front line and can always be approached on any issue. We find effective communications with the community – schools, parents and students. Powerful messages have been sent and received. Staff in The Learning Trust never shirked from having courageous conversations with schools when necessary.

Celebration

[39]Hargreaves, A. & Fink, D. (2006) Sustainable Leadership. San Francisco: Jossey-Bass

[40]The Guardian, 2 November 2010.

Shirley Williams (Baroness Williams of Crosby) chaired the national Teaching Awards panel from 2006–2010. Two things strike her as important. First that all winners say 'It isn't for me; it's for my team.' And second they are self-confident and not worried about drawing attention to themselves.[40] Before Lord Puttnam introduced the Teaching Awards in 1998, celebrating good teaching seemed to be something alien to our culture. This was still true in Hackney when The Learning Trust started in 2002. Since then they have changed the culture. We learn how the Trust used celebration and rewards as a deliberate strategy to acknowledge the achievements of students, teachers and other professionals in schools and within The Learning Trust. Through high profile events and high quality publications, the Trust spread good news about Hackney education through the local community and beyond. It had an important impact on building confidence within the community as well as the workforce. It was no surprise to find a Hackney headteacher won the National Headteacher of the Year award in 2009.

Consistency

In Leadership for Mortals, Dean Fink presents a model for leadership succession which sorts five components into two groups: those that should never change and those that should always change.[41] The two components that should never change are commitment and values. We learn how The Learning Trust consistently upheld its values and commitment throughout its contract. In doing so, we find that succession planning is underway to safeguard progress and ensure continued improvements as the administration returns to Hackney Council.

[41] Fink, D. (2005)
Leadership for Mortals.
London: Paul Chapman
Publishing

Concept

*Even very young children need to be informed about
dying. Explain the concept of death very carefully
to your child. This will make threatening him with it
much more effective.*
                                        P. J. O'Rourke

We consider the political situation at Government
level and learn how decisions were made to intervene
in order to remove education from Hackney Council's
administration. The Learning Trust is a unique
organisation that was never copied during the ten
year contract. The independence of The Learning Trust
helped significantly. Mike Tomlinson, the first Chair
of the Board of Directors energised the organisation
and schools improved rapidly. The Board's vision and
strategy were clear from the outset. The Learning Trust
soon established a high-performance culture within
the organisation that is widely shared by its employees.
We reveal the concept of The Learning Trust as it exists
today by describing its key features.

Secretary of State for Education and Skills, Estelle
Morris remembers the political situation leading up to
the Government's intervention in Hackney Council.[42]

[42] Estelle Morris was
Secretary of State for
Education and Skills
from 2001 – 2002,
at the start of the
Blair government's
second term of office.
She had been a
Government minister
in the Department
for Education and
Employment during
Labour's first term
of office from 1997 –
2001. As Secretary of
State, Estelle Morris
was responsible for
establishing The
Learning Trust.

66 There were a number of threads at the time.
One is going into the second term of the Labour
Government when the priority was school
improvement and raising standards. Some
members of the Government had an equivocal
view of local authorities. I think the Prime Minister
might have preferred to take education out of local
government altogether. I'm not saying that he
put that forward but I think he was a huge sceptic
about local authorities and education but that
wasn't the policy. 99

Estelle Morris: Secretary of State for Education and Skills
2001–2002

In its first term of office (1997–2001) the Labour Government had already passed legislation that enabled it to intervene in education and Ofsted's responsibilities had been extended to inspect local education authorities. These were early days in terms of local authority intervention.

> Trying to work with local authorities that were under-achieving was a new policy at the time. We had just started to inspect LEAs and the first interventions followed. Nobody had dealt with under-performing local authorities before. They had just dealt with under-performing schools. Because of the democratic accountability of local authorities, people had thought they ought not to deal with them.
>
> Estelle Morris: Secretary of State for Education and Skills 2001–2002

Part of the context at the time was the fact that the Prime Minister, Tony Blair, did not send his own children to his local secondary school in the London borough of Islington. We may deduce that this was because secondary schools in Islington were well below the national average in terms of their GCSE and A-level results. Whatever the reason, the performance of schools in Islington and other inner London boroughs was always seized on by the national press in order to hold to account the Prime Minister who had professed his three priorities in Government were 'education, education and education.'[43] Estelle Morris, Secretary of State for Education at the time highlights this.

[43] BBC News Talking Point: 'Should the prime minister be turning to private tutors?' 10 July 2002 http://news.bbc.co.uk/1/hi/talking_point/2097355.stm

> Wrongly, the press tends to write the Government's education policy up as it exists in London. So Hackney and Islington were the two big stories. They were always the worst schools in the country. We wanted to improve those areas but we knew that until we did improve them nobody would ever recognise the good work that was going on in places like Knowsley and elsewhere.

Estelle Morris: Secretary of State for Education and Skills 2001–2002

However, the press was right about Hackney Council. As we have already described in our section that sets the scene, problems were piling up and schools were under-performing. Naturally the Government was concerned.

> Hackney was always on our mind. It was troublesome in so many areas. It never went off our political agenda.

Estelle Morris: Secretary of State for Education and Skills 2001–2002

At the time, education was the only aspect of local government subject to rigorous evaluation and intervention by national Government when things fell apart.

> There was no other Government department that was dealing with local authority under performance. In those days we didn't have Joint Area Reviews or anything like that. At the Department for Education and Skills we were leading the way in terms of under-performing local authorities. The minute we started intervening, Hackney and Islington needed to be top of the list. All the messages from Ofsted were that they could not be saved.

Estelle Morris: Secretary of State for Education and Skills 2001–2002

Pioneering its new policy, the Government was learning as it went along. Initial interventions tended to be cautious, as it was with the first intervention in Hackney.

66 We let a contract, the way we were experimenting at the time, to a private company (Nord Anglia). It was so bureaucratic. I remember Chris Woodhead (Her Majesty's Chief Inspector of schools) rightly pointing out that one of their measures was that the telephone should not ring more than six times before it was answered. With all the problems that faced Hackney, why should we be concerned about how long it took to answer the telephone? I'm not saying that's not important but that's how paranoid we were about everything in the contract. We were learning. 99

Estelle Morris: Secretary of State for Education and Skills 2001–2002

By the time the problems in Hackney Council reached the critical level in 2000, the Government's Department for Education and Skills already had several years' experience of interventions in other places such as Bradford, Walsall, Islington and Southwark. Education ministers were much more robust in their attitude towards intervention than their Cabinet colleagues. Estelle Morris explains:

> We had this meeting which looked at Hackney as a
> local authority and they (Government colleagues)
> were almost saying 'Give them a warning and a
> bit more help'. We were desperate really because
> Nord Anglia hadn't worked. The rest of the
> Government departments wanted to do something
> about Hackney but their minds and their policy
> was not where we were. Out of it all came The
> Learning Trust which protected education
> in Hackney from the organisational failures
> elsewhere in the local authority.

Estelle Morris: Secretary of State for Education and Skills
2001–2002

Unlike other local authorities such as Walsall, where the
Council welcomed intervention, in Hackney there was
no such willingness.[44] The intervention was imposed
by Government. The current Chief Executive of Hackney
Council explains.

> In November 2001, Hackney Council was given
> 21 directions by the Government. One of these
> directions was to set up a body which took
> responsibility for the delivery of education in the
> borough. It was mandated, we had to do it, and
> it was mandated that we would have to do it by a
> certain date, which was done.

Tim Shields: Chief Executive Hackney Council

The structure of The Learning Trust was unique and
remains so. The option of transferring the schools to
another local authority was rejected. A contract with
a private company was the preferred solution but
there was concern about private companies making
a profit from running what was previously a public
service.[45] The argument was simple, why divert money
allocated for children's education as profit to the
shareholders of a private company? The solution was
a private not-for-profit company solely charged with

[44] Walsall Council Cabinet
Minutes: 19 January
2005, Agenda item 7,
Education Walsall

[45] BBC News 'New Trust to
run education service.'
17 October 2001. http://
news.bbc.co.uk/1/hi/
england/1604074.stm

education in Hackney. Instead of shareholders, the Board of The Learning Trust was responsible to Hackney Council which was acting on behalf of the residents in the borough. Instead of making financial profit, The Learning Trust was motivated by making intellectual profit in terms of the educational outcomes of young people in Hackney. Places on the Board of non-executive directors were reserved for the Mayor, Chief Executive and Lead Member for children's services of Hackney Council. Other places were allocated to headteachers, governors and other stakeholders in the community.[46] The three executive directors on the Board are: Chief Executive, Director of Learning and Standards and Director of Finance and Resources.

The length of the contract was an important consideration. Evidence from Ofsted shows that failing schools may be turned around in under two years but that depends to some extent on how bad they are to begin with.[47] It takes longer to create sustainable improvements that produce outstanding schools. Systemic change takes longer still.[48] We also know that any change process will be bumpy. Taking all this into consideration, a ten year contract was probably the minimum length of time to give The Learning Trust a reasonable chance to show success.

[46] Composition of The Learning Trust Board http://trustnet. learningtrust.co.uk/ Trust/company/Pages/ TheBoard.aspx

[47] Ofsted (1999) Lessons learned from special measures. London: Ofsted

[48] Michael Fullan writes extensively about leadership and change in education. See 'All Systems Go' (2010) Corwin Press

> We knew from the early contracts that it couldn't be three or five years. By the time we got to The Learning Trust we decided to lengthen it even further.
>
> Estelle Morris: Secretary of State for Education and Skills 2001–2002

Appointing Sir Mike Tomlinson as the first Chair of The Learning Trust was a stroke of genius. He was approaching retirement from his post as Her Majesty's Chief Inspector of schools and head of Ofsted, after a highly successful and distinguished career in education.

> Mike had the experience and respect we needed.
> His career was at a point where we could take
> him out and ask him to do it. The fact that he
> came from Ofsted helped because nobody could
> criticise him as being weak on evaluation or
> frightened to be tough on schools. He was about
> to retire but he was in good health and keen to do
> it. He was at a stage in his career where he was
> going to go in and take charge. He didn't have any
> cares about his next promotion. He had stature
> and confidence.
>
> Estelle Morris: Secretary of State for Education and Skills
> 2001–2002

Once again we see that The Learning Trust broke the
mould in terms of privatising education services in
England. Not only was it a not-for-profit company but its
leader had devoted his entire career to education rather
than business. This was an important factor that got
things off to a flying start.

> By putting Mike in charge we were going back to our
> tried and tested educationalists, people like him
> who have credibility. We were trying to get school
> improvement in, not destroy the local authority.
> We wanted a non-profit motive and to keep some
> semblance of local democracy. But more than
> that, the golden rule was it had to be allowed to
> get on with improving education and could not be
> held back by failures elsewhere. We were trying
> to isolate it from the local authority but leave it
> enmeshed in the local community. The Learning
> Trust was the vehicle we chose to do that.
>
> Estelle Morris: Secretary of State for Education and Skills
> 2001–2002

Mike's appointment was immediately welcomed by
schools in Hackney, as indicated by a secondary
headteacher at the time.

> What gave it (The Learning Trust) street credibility and professional respectability was the fact that it was based on sound educational practice. It wasn't based on a political forum, it wasn't based on the Council wanting to do this or somebody wanting to do that or what was the cheapest way of doing things. It was based on sound educational principles. It also allowed people to take risks because remember there was nothing to lose prior to that time.

Jenny Wilkins: Principal Skinners' Academy

Mike left Ofsted in March 2002 and planned to spend the summer watching cricket before The Learning Trust contract began in September of that year. However, things didn't quite work out that way and he was soon spending most of his time in Hackney in the lead up to the transfer of administration from the Council. One of his first tasks was to get a board appointed.

> The board was hugely representative of the local community including: headteachers, governors, local business people and the superintendent of police. We chose businesses, such as UBS, which already had links with Hackney schools. There was a synergy about it and in the end we got a board that was wide-ranging in its composition in terms of the community at large and also single-minded. The single-mindedness was that we were concerned with one thing and one thing only – education in Hackney from the cradle to the grave.

Sir Mike Tomlinson: first Chair of The Learning Trust

Mike quickly established an inspirational dream that everyone in Hackney wanted more than anything else: that in ten year's time parents would be struggling to get places for their children in Hackney secondary

schools. In 2002, this was almost unimaginable; it was
achieved by 2010.

> All I did was set out where I wanted us to be. This
> is what I want us to do and this is how I am going
> to play my part in it. 'I believe that at the end of
> this journey you are going to be proud to work
> in Hackney. People are going to recognise you
> because you work in Hackney.'

Sir Mike Tomlinson: first Chair of The Learning Trust

Mike's message was immediately welcomed by many
good people in Hackney schools who were doing
the best they could at the time. As in many failing
organisations it is easy to neglect the strengths it
has because they are so heavily outweighed by the
weaknesses. While the council had struggled to
support school improvement, there were some good
schools and good features in other schools.

> In those difficult circumstances of being left
> without support, most headteachers, even if they
> weren't capable of raising standards and running
> a good school, had a high protection over the
> community. So they were quite pastoral, they
> looked after the children and kept them safe. What
> some of them didn't understand was the journey
> to give them better quality teaching to get better
> outcomes, at that point in time.

Tricia Okoruwa: Deputy Director The Learning Trust

Alan Wood became Chief Executive of The Learning
Trust and provided the vital leadership to establish a
positive relationship between The Learning Trust and
the schools in Hackney.

> ❝ There wasn't really a relationship between the council and the schools. There was very little guidance. We (headteachers) used to laugh about things; it was the only way to keep sane. We had a different slogan every year and a folder would come out with it on but with no plan as to how you would actually get there. ❞
>
> Tricia Okoruwa: primary school headteacher at the time

By comparison, the vision shared by Mike Tomlinson and Alan Wood was not just a slogan, as Alan makes clear.

> ❝ The refusal to accept low standards wasn't just exaltation, it was an action. ❞
>
> Alan Wood: Chief Executive The Learning Trust

The Learning Trust immediately realised that the vacuum left by the Council gave them a great opportunity to make a difference. The current Chair of the board explains.

> ❝ The level of education in Hackney had reached such a low point that there wasn't anybody in the firm who didn't believe that improvement was possible. So we had a very promising start. The executive directors never had any doubt that we could achieve what we needed to achieve. I thought history could be created here in terms of the transformation of prospects for young people compared to what had been before. ❞
>
> Richard Hardie: Chair of The Learning Trust

The single-mindedness that gave expression to the board's determination to raise standards was also apparent in the work of The Learning Trust. Unlike Hackney Council which had responsibility for the administration of other public services, The Learning Trust had a single focus – education. This was an important feature of its success as several people explain.

> The focus of The Learning Trust as an organisation has been entirely on education, providing support services, leadership and governance. We have not had additional responsibilities around more corporate local authority activities. That focus on education is one of several reasons for our ability to improve education in Hackney.

Alan Wood: Chief Executive The Learning Trust

> As an organisation, The Learning Trust is smaller than the Council and we're here only for one reason and that was defined in the beginning. That helped because there was a focus on the outcomes.

Ann Seago: Senior Family Information Officer The Learning Trust

> I certainly think that having a body with a single focus on education has been a good thing. The Council has taken that approach with some services. Sometimes it has decided to outsource something to give somebody a single focus to deal with an issue. Later on it has brought it back in-house again. Sometimes it makes sense to park something with someone else who has a single focus for improvement.

Tim Shields: Chief Executive Hackney Council

The Learning Trust adopted a traditional hierarchical approach to its leadership and management style. That emerges from conversations with the current chair of the board and senior executive directors. It has been argued that this is the most effective style in a turnaround situation where weaknesses outnumber strengths.[49]

[49] Leithwood, Jantzi and Steinbach (2000), Changing Leadership for Changing Times. Milton Keynes: Open University Press

" In terms of the way the firm has been run, it's been like any other business that I've worked for. In essence a company needs a vision. It needs a strategy for achieving that vision. It needs to empower its managers to implement the strategy and it has to ensure that they have the resources to do it. It also has to have processes in place to test whether that strategy has been achieved or not. That's a set of guiding principles that have been applied here but I don't claim credit for it. There was a collective will to have in place structures that gave a real sense of belonging and purpose to everybody who was in the firm. "

Richard Hardie: Chair of The Learning Trust

" There was no question at all that it was top-down, but it didn't feel as though you were being marginalised, you weren't being told everything. There was a facilitation to have a dialogue about what it would look like without the blame culture being attached to it. "

Tricia Okoruwa: primary school headteacher at the time

" Because of the way we are structured, I can make sure that we're totally joined up in Human Resources, Legal, Governor Services or whatever. I can make sure that we're all supporting each other with the task in hand. In a local authority you have different corporate directors ruling different parts and that makes it more difficult. "

Steve Belk: Director of Learning and Standards The Learning Trust

In the beginning improving secondary schools was the main priority for fairly obvious reasons.

> We knew the first thing we needed to improve was secondary for a number of reasons. Not just the examination results but also the fact that at the time 40% of 11 year-olds opted out of the borough for their secondary education. Almost without exception, those were parents we actually wanted with us in the system. We wanted them to be the catalysts for change, who demanded something better than they were getting before.

Sir Mike Tomlinson: first Chair of The Learning Trust

> What we knew at the very beginning was the disquiet and unrest among the local community of parents. The quality of some secondary schools was poor. There were not enough places for boys because we had so many girls' schools and also a preponderance of faith schools. Many things about secondary provision didn't work for parents.
>
> So from the start there was a clear strategy around both the improvement of secondary provision and the rationalisation of additional places. That played out in two ways which joined when we closed poorly performing schools and replaced them with new schools that would provide a better balance to the places available. There was a very explicit school improvement agenda.

Elaine Peers: Head of partnerships and safeguarding, former head of school place planning The Learning Trust

It was important to engage with secondary headteachers in order to develop and implement a secondary strategy. Because it was clear that some schools would be closed, it was vital for The Learning Trust to establish its integrity with the group of secondary heads. This was a challenging situation and the approach is outlined by the Chief Executive:

> We had a very clear secondary strategy which you can take all the way back to 2002 when we had a meeting with all heads of secondary schools and colleges. We had a discussion about what the future was. I started the discussion by passing round a report to the Department for Education from the Chief Inspector of schools following a visit to Hackney schools five years hence. The future was laid out in the form of a report. It spoke about new schools, it spoke about high performances and investment.
>
> Our secondary strategy was underpinned by three clear priorities:
>
> 1. Improve standards – recruit quality consultants; recruit quality leadership. Improving our existing schools was the first priority.
>
> 2. Invest in existing schools – through the Building Schools for the Future programme, we invested £170 – 200 million in our existing secondary schools.[50]
>
> 3. Increase the number of places – the only way to achieve this was through the Academies programme.[51]

Alan Wood: Chief Executive The Learning Trust

[50] Building Schools for the Future (BSF) was an ambitious programme to rebuild state schools across England. Initiated in 2005 by the Labour government, it was intended to spend £45 billion over 15 to 20 years. BSF was partly financed by the private sector in return for ongoing maintenance contracts for the new buildings. The programme was cancelled by the coalition government in 2011 to reduce the Government budget deficit.

[51] Academies are secondary schools funded directly by the Government. They are independent of local authorities but may be sponsored by a private company, individual or foundation. They were established by the Labour government in 2000 and the Government made it clear to local authorities that if they wanted to build a new secondary school then it would have to be an academy.

Building five brand new academies in Hackney between 2002-2011 is even more impressive than the construction of the Olympic park at Stratford. Combined with the Building Schools for the Future (BSF) programme, The Learning Trust has completely transformed the secondary school provision in Hackney. None of this could be achieved without a strong partnership with Hackney Council. However, the Chief Executive's three strategic priorities above are listed in order of impact on GCSE results. The GCSE results in Hackney schools improved steadily from

2002–2011, moving above the national average in 2009, when only the first of the new academies had students in Year 11 and therefore made a contribution to the borough average.

Embracing the Academy programme was expedient rather than philosophical. While it is hardly surprising that a private company would commit itself to setting up a string of independent schools, the fact that The Learning Trust was able to engage full support from Hackney Council is evidence of its commitment to a set of guiding principles. Those involved in the programme tell the story.

> Our strategy was to provide places for 80% of the pupil population.[52] In order to move to that level from where we were, we knew we had to build new schools in the right locations. We wanted places for every parent who wanted to send their children to a Hackney school. But in order to achieve that, they had to be high quality.

Elaine Peers: Head of partnerships and safeguarding, former head of school place planning The Learning Trust

> The authority had no money for capital expenditure and it was clear that the Government was not going to give them any credits. The first thing we had to do was draw together a secondary development plan. If we wanted new places that could only be in 'academy land'. That was the only way we were going to get new schools and increase the places available. We prepared a policy document which spelled out our aspirations for secondary both in terms of the number of schools and the geographic location of schools. We said that this would be somewhere in the order of a five-year plan.

Sir Mike Tomlinson: first Chair of The Learning Trust

[52] Based on the statistical projection that 20% of the student population would be educated elsewhere.

"When it first came up about academies, people were nervous, wary and against it. What we (The Learning Trust) made clear was that we wouldn't support any academy that wasn't committed to Hackney. We were very clear about the criteria for what we would accept and what they (the sponsors) would agree to. There was never going to be any money to build a school so it was the only way forward for us. The reason Hackney can boast the most successful academy programme is because the attitude of the Trust to finding the right sponsors. All the sponsors are clearly dedicated to Hackney which makes a difference."

Peter Passam: Governor of the Best Start Federation; the strategic management board of the federated PRU & non-executive director The Learning Trust

"We had three criteria for anybody coming in to sponsor an academy:

1. We were not interested in being sponsored by a religious body, as a multi-ethnic authority and all that goes with that.

2. They had to be non-selective and a member of the family of Hackney schools. We didn't want those who became islands unto themselves, or those who wouldn't cooperate.

3. Sponsors should have an existing link with Hackney."

Sir Mike Tomlinson: first Chair of The Learning Trust

> ❝ We didn't follow the model that some other boroughs had, where you closed the school and immediately opened it as a new school with a different name but in the same buildings. We took the view that in order to have sustainable school improvement across all schools we needed to completely close the school and start a new school from fresh. The first four academies followed that model where they started from Year 7 and increased their roll incrementally. ❞

Elaine Peers: Head of partnerships and safeguarding, former head of school place planning The Learning Trust

> ❝ The Council was heavily involved in setting up the academies. The strategy was about not having re-treads. They were all new builds, new headteachers, all of those things. We provided clean sites for new builds. We were not transitioning from a failing school into an academy. That was quite a brave step and so far it has paid off. ❞

Tim Shields: Chief Executive Hackney Council

Finding space to build new schools in London is difficult. In an area as densely populated as Hackney it is impossible. Every square metre of land available has been built on or is protected. The only possibility is to clear an existing site. The Learning Trust wasted no time in moving ahead to build the first academy, Mossbourne, on the Hackney Downs site. This was a typically brave decision by The Learning Trust given the controversy over the closure of Hackney Downs. Mossbourne opened for Year 7 pupils in September 2004.

Although bold, that first step was easier than the next which was to close existing schools and move the students elsewhere in order to free up the space to build new academies. The Learning Trust quickly demonstrated its zero-tolerance approach to school failure.

> 66 There were two secondary schools which had been in special measures.[53] One had been in special measures for some years and had not improved. It was in danger of becoming a sink school for African Caribbean pupils only. The other was poorly performing. Both schools had lost parental support as well as their credibility. We did not want to create an academy that transferred across any of the students from those schools. We wanted academies to start from scratch so they weren't inheriting a whole pack of historical problems. That was challenging as it meant decanting those students. We got a lot of cooperation from existing secondary schools, a lot of cooperation with bordering authorities and we set up a temporary school within the FE college. 99
>
> Sir Mike Tomlinson: first Chair of The Learning Trust

> 66 The Learning Trust did not move away from making the difficult decisions. 99
>
> Cheryl Day: Headteacher Clapton Girls' Technology College

The academy programme was also threatening to the existing secondary schools that were doing well at the time. The Learning Trust worked hard to avoid creating a two-tier system by ensuring the sponsors of the new academies were committed to the Hackney community and to working in partnership with the other schools. Nevertheless, the other secondary schools clearly need to show they were not inferior in any way. Mike Tomlinson explains how this was built into the strategy.

[53] Schools that fail an Ofsted inspection require 'special measures'. The term refers to a range of interventions and intense monitoring that continues until the school provides a satisfactory standard of education, as judged by Ofsted.

> If the strategy had been adopted where pupils were transferred into the academy, the new school would have produced GCSE results quite quickly. We wanted to give the remaining secondary schools five years at least to get ready for what was coming. If they (the academies) did take pupils from the two schools being closed and their results were better than the other schools then you know what would follow. It was quite deliberate on our part.

Sir Mike Tomlinson: first Chair of The Learning Trust

By 2011 The Learning Trust has secured a collaborative ethos among the secondary schools in which all the schools want to play their part in Hackney's overall success. Naturally, they want their school to be better than the one down the road but this is about professional pride and not just about attracting the highest achieving pupils from primary schools. The fact that these schools, taking mainly pupils from low income families, perform above the national averages turns the belief that poverty is no excuse for school failure into reality. They are beacons of hope for everyone.

> Once you get more schools succeeding then you're raising expectations. There was a general acceptance in secondary that children from a poor background can do well. Prior to that a lot of school improvement was about trying to get the better students rather than all students doing well. Now there is this collective ambition.

Steve Belk: Director of Learning and Standards The Learning Trust

While secondary schools were the first priority, The Learning Trust did not ignore the primary sector which was far more complex. It was not just that there are more primary schools that made it complicated.

Primary schools are the front line of the education system when it comes to dealing with the grim realities of life in deprived communities. Teachers who choose to work in high poverty schools deserve respect from our society. But more than that, those children deserve the best education that we can provide because they need it more than anyone else.

There have always been some outstanding primary schools in Hackney and that was true in 2002 when the Learning Trust was established. At that point there were also a high number of primary schools with identified serious weaknesses and just as many where the weaknesses had not been revealed by Ofsted. The big difference is that by 2011 there are many more outstanding primary schools and none with serious weaknesses. The improvement strategy in primary schools is an intriguing blend of short-term and long-term strategies as revealed by the Deputy Director who joined The Learning Trust in 2004.

> Early on I realised it had to be in two parts – predict & prevent, and find & fix. At the beginning there wasn't enough resource to be able to do both of these elements which is probably why the primary results took a bit longer to come through. It was always going to be around sustainability, it was never quick fix. So we put a big investment into the early years, into key stage 1 and into literacy.[54] To get kids reading by age seven was one of the key parts of the strategy. This was the 'predict and prevent' part. We know all about deprivation and the community we serve.
>
> The 'find and fix' bit was looking at the schools where the results were not so good. Analysing the data scrupulously and getting in there to work with Years 5 and 6.[55] This helped to accelerate pupils' learning. We used things like: booster

[54] Early years refers to pre-school provision in nursery and reception classes. Key stage 1 covers Years 1 and 2 for students aged 5–7.

[55] National tests are taken by all students at the end of Year 6 (age 11).

classes, breakfast clubs, after-school coaching and summer schemes. We still do some of that because some of our kids still need the additional support, but not on the same scale that we used to do. 99

Tricia Okoruwa: Deputy Director The Learning Trust

There was a great deal of fire-fighting in primary schools when The Learning Trust started to support schools. The danger was that this would overwhelm the organisation and prevent it from recognising the need to put strategies in place that would secure sustainable improvements, let alone actually implementing them. Even so, 'find and fix' far outweighed 'predict and prevent' in terms of time and energy for the first five years. The head of the inclusion team explains.

66 If Ofsted was coming, during the first three years of The Learning Trust, we all stayed whole weekends in schools putting stuff up. All that's changed. We realised that schools came out with a better judgment but actually we then still had to go back and do all the support because it wasn't there really and we knew it. But now we're far more honest and transparent. We've realised that we've got some good headteachers who know how they want their school to improve. 99

Lizzie Yauner: Head of inclusion team The Learning Trust

Looking at the situation overall, it was clear that The Learning Trust made significant improvements in both primary and secondary to begin with. That was essential because the initial standards were so low and although not easy, there was a lot of space to move into. Pushing the schools further ahead required a step-change in terms of strategy and support. The Director of Learning and Standards points this out:

> Mid-way through we started to develop a joined-up strategy for primary and secondary; then we shifted another gear. We created an ambition that we wanted all schools to be good or better. We concentrated on improving learning and teaching. This became central to our strategy, making sure that we were building capacity rather than applying quick fixes.
>
> Steve Belk: Director of Learning and Standards The Learning Trust

In this section we have tried to capture the beliefs, the principles and the practices that characterise The Learning Trust's work in Hackney and describe the concept of this way of working. We should stress that it is not just the concept which is important but also the consistency in the way it has been developed and used. We learn from this research that consistency is an important feature in its own right so we report about it in a separate section. The remarkable improvements in Hackney were achieved when the powerful concept we have outlined here was applied consistently.

Given the success that has been achieved, two things surprise us. One is that the organisation remains unique, it has not been copied. The other is that after ten years' outstanding success, when the contract ends in 2012, The Learning Trust itself will cease to exist. Maybe it has done its job and now it is time to move on.

> From the start I always had confidence that with the right people in the right positions this was a model that really offered an opportunity for a lot of places, not just in Hackney. I'm amazed it hasn't happened anywhere else.
>
> Peter Passam: Governor of the Best Start Federation; the strategic management board of the federated PRU & non-executive director The Learning Trust

The chief executive of Hackney Council has been a member of The Learning Trust board throughout its existence. The Council is fully aware of the reasons for the outstanding improvements and is determined that they will continue when the Council takes over administration of education in 2012.

> One of the things we've (the Council) got to do is make sure that whatever governance arrangements are in place they are at strategic level and we don't get into the detail. Getting these arrangements right, whether there's a board or whatever it is, that's critical to the success going forward.
>
> Tim Shields: Chief Executive Hackney Council

Capacity

Leadership is the wise use of power. Power is the capacity to translate intention into reality and sustain it.
Warren G Bennis

We use the word 'capacity' to describe the collective abilities, skills, intellectual understanding and resources within The Learning Trust and Hackney schools that is used to help students learn. While resources such as time, the number of people and the finance available may be fixed, we take the view that the abilities, skills and intellectual understanding in any organisation is unlimited and offers potential for growth. What we find from our study is how The Learning Trust was able to significantly increase the capacity across schools in Hackney and also within the organisation itself. It was through increased capacity that schools were able to improve students' achievements as indicated by GCSE results and national test scores.

As we delved deeper into the ways that The Learning Trust set about building capacity in Hackney, we found four strands that are so powerful in terms of capacity building that we decided to report on them separately. We have called these separate strands: Challenge; Courage; Creativity and Collaboration and each one is described in a separate section. These are vital components for school improvement.

The Learning Trust inherited a failing education system from Hackney Council in 2002. Some education services had been taken out of the Council's control in 1999 when Nord Anglia had taken on the contract to run the School Improvement Service for the next three years. Despite this, capacity was very low because many key posts were vacant and also in terms of the collective abilities across the entire workforce.

An education officer appointed by Hackney Council remembers.

> The day I started working in Hackney the Director and Deputy Director of education both resigned. I tried not to take it personally, but in a sense that was the most obvious symptom of the political disarray of the council at the time.

Neil Weeks: Corporate Governance Officer The Learning Trust

Obtaining information about the schools and how they were doing seemed to be an impossible task. The Trust had little if any reliable data to go on beside the statutory end of key stage and GCSE results. They did not know how or where individual schools required help. There was nothing built in to the system to help identify or outline areas for school improvement. The Director of Learning and Standards gives us an insight.

> There was no secondary improvement service when I came. There was 'Excellence in Cities' which was a government initiative but there was no consistent school improvement process.[56] There was no way to support all schools and no way to gain intelligence of all that.

Steve Belk: Director of Learning and Standards
The Learning Trust

The Learning Trust soon recognised that some staff had outlived their usefulness and that the organisation had no room for them. This was all part of the Trust's refusal to accept second best and it is a clear illustration of why courage is essential in order to build capacity.[57]

[56] Excellence in Cities was a Government initiative introduced in 1999 to improve secondary education in inner city areas. The programme was centrally prescribed and funded. It was evaluated by Ofsted in 2005 and the report may be downloaded from www.ofsted.gov.uk/resources/excellence-cities-managing-associated- initiatives-raise-standards

[57] Courage is dealt with in more depth in another section of this report; see contents for page reference.

> When you come into an organisation you find out who the people are and you work with them and try to build the organisation. At the same point they may have reached their peak and the organisation moves beyond them and then you have to deal with that.
>
> Steve Belk: Director of Learning and Standards
> The Learning Trust

In order to get things moving in Hackney, the Trust needed to hire a lot of external consultants. While some consultants made significant contributions, it became apparent that others regarded Hackney as a lost cause. They took the attitude that the people working in it were incapable and possibly to blame for the state that Hackney education was in. This did not help the atmosphere within the Trust.

> In the early days of the Learning Trust there was an over reliance on external consultants. The idea prevailed that no one in Hackney could do a good job. A lot of these people who did come in, many of them from the private sector, came in with a negative attitude of what happened. They had heard all the rumours and they did regard people who had worked in Hackney for many years as being incompetent, inefficient not knowing what they were doing. The irony is those people didn't last long here. It's the people who have worked here for a long time who have made the difference.
>
> Neil Weeks: Corporate Governance Officer The Learning Trust

The Trust had employed these consultants at great expense and for very little gain in overall capacity. It retained the staff who were good at their jobs. There was a strategy for improvement but the big question was how to build sufficient capacity to implement the strategy without further adding to the financial burden? The answer was to develop the capacity from within. There were some highly respected, effective and motivated people working within The Learning Trust. The solution was to use these skilled people, develop and train them to be even better and in the process show that the Trust had faith in its staff. This illustrates the creativity and risk-taking that enabled The Learning Trust to increase capacity.[58] One of the current Deputy Directors of The Learning Trust was a primary headteacher when she was headhunted by the Trust.

> He (the Director) said to me that after looking at the situation and the history, because he knew the context really well, having been a head at Stoke Newington School, the solution has got to come from within Hackney. Not by bringing people in. It was a big risk because although I knew how to run a good school, I didn't know anything about system reform. I had to learn quickly how to affect change across other schools.
>
> Tricia Okoruwa: Deputy Director The Learning Trust

This was a typically bold move by the Trust as they were able to match specific people to areas where they knew they would be most effective.

Recruiting headteachers and deputies in schools was a big challenge for school governing bodies. The quality of applicants for posts was poor and those that came didn't stay long. In the same way, the Trust wanted to support those good staff already committed to working in Hackney schools and train them to become leaders.

[58] Creativity is dealt with in more depth in another section of this report; see contents for page reference.

❝ We had to grow our own future leaders and develop a programme of support for aspiring heads and deputies. We also needed to build up school capacity for improvement. ❞

Sir Mike Tomlinson: first Chair of The Learning Trust

Those identified as having the potential to become leaders, either a head or a deputy, were encouraged to join the Aspiring Leaders programme. Similarly, the middle management of the schools was also developed; it really was about succession planning. Today the Learning Trust's leadership programme is an extensive one:

- Leadership conferences to address issues of leadership, including a residential conference for headteachers

- Bespoke training and support for new and acting headteachers

- Residential conference for deputy and assistant headteachers

- Senior leadership training for deputy and assistant headteachers

- Network meetings for NQT co-ordinators

- Succession training, a pilot for primary leaders in conjunction with the NCSL that also has a focus on increasing the numbers applying for leadership positions in faith schools and to increase the number of leaders of Black and Minority Ethnic heritage;

- Pre and Post NPQH Leadership Development opportunities for aspiring leaders of schools with a religious character and/ or leaders of Black and Minority Ethnic heritage – we are working in partnership with NCSL to provide a programme of Targeted Support for pre- NPQH and post-NPQH graduates who aspire to headship in the next five years. This programme will be funded and will include workshops, mentoring and coaching.

- Leadership development opportunities for aspiring leaders of Black and Minority Ethnic heritage will also be offered in collaboration with NCSL.

- Middle leadership meetings for subject practitioners, SENCOs, strategy managers and other specialist post holders;

- Training for newly appointed or aspiring middle leaders are offered in conjunction with the London Centre for Leadership and Learning.

- Courses on current issues, many of which are linked to the 'Every Child Matters' agenda and the development of children's services in Hackney.

(A full list of professional learning opportunities is available on The Learning Trust website)

> For me what's been really powerful is the professional development I've received from The Learning Trust. They said 'You've got the potential' and I was invited onto the Aspiring Leaders programme. What I was learning I could actually take back into schools, but I felt really trusted as well. What amazed me, because I've got friends who do similar jobs to me in other authorities, is how flexible the working is here and also the trust and the opportunity to be innovative.
>
> Bukky Yusuf: Senior science consultant The Learning Trust

By growing its own talent, The Learning Trust has increased the leadership capacity in Hackney over the last ten years. This has improved the recruitment pool for schools as this governor recognises.

> ❝ There was a lack of quality headteachers out there so for the past few years the Trust has been developing this leadership programme. You've got to be of the belief that you can't settle for second best – I would rather not appoint than put in someone that is second best. ❞
>
> Peter Passam: Governor of the Best Start Federation; the strategic management board of the federated PRU & non-executive director The Learning Trust

Before The Learning Trust was established, schools relied on their own capacity for improvement. Large secondary schools had sufficient capacity to organise their own professional learning (CPD) which explains why some secondary schools were improving well before 2002.

> ❝ The school has great deliverers of INSET who are actually outstanding teachers so they have the credibility. ❞
>
> Cheryl Day: Headteacher Clapton Girls' Technology College

However, this was not the case in many primary schools. The Deputy Director contrasts what it was like in 2002 with the situation today.

> ❝ There was no succession planning. The schools that were doing well, like Lauriston and Jubilee, were doing good CPD. But apart from these there was no strategy around it. Most teachers were surviving as well as those heads. It was go in, do your best and hope that nothing awful happens or that the Ofsted call wouldn't come.
>
> Initially the replacement heads came from outside the borough. Since then we have developed new leadership through internal programmes. We didn't get people applying to Hackney for their

second headship until about three years ago and that was quite significant that people were choosing to come to Hackney for their second headship. That was a bit of a test that the status and reputation had changed. Good people applying from our neighbouring boroughs was a clear signal that the word on the street was that things were getting better.

The selection method of staff has also become more effective – more focus on essential things. These are some of the key leadership skills we've learned to look for. First can they self–manage? Are they resilient? And can they hold people to account? We have become more precise about what it is and also about recognising where the school is at. We are better at appointing the right Head with the right skills for the stage of development of the school. 99

Tricia Okoruwa: Deputy Director The Learning Trust

The policy of planning for future leaders and growing them from within the borough has been very successful. Good staff are rewarded by being moved up the leadership ladder whether it is at senior or middle management level.

So far we have considered how The Trust developed capacity through support. We also find that The Trust put a great emphasis on using its School Improvement Partners to challenge schools.[59]

In 2004 the DfES and Ofsted set out a vision for a new relationship between government and schools. The introduction of a School Improvement Partner was intended to release greater local initiative and energy in schools and help them to raise educational standards. The School Improvement Partner, who was in many cases someone with current or recent headship

[59] Challenge is dealt with in more depth in another section of this report; see contents for page r eference.

experience, acted as the conduit between The Learning Trust and the school, helping set targets and priorities and identifying support needed. This led to more joined-up working within The Learning Trust and a more efficient way of working.

The robust relationship with schools also made a significant contribution to capacity building. This was an innovative role to provide expert support to schools in their drive to raise standards and improve the education of all pupils.

> It was about finding out the needs of individual schools then putting together a big picture and seeing how we could best pool our resources to support that. We joined up together so school improvement had oversight of all the areas. If it was a human resource issue then it would automatically trigger an input from school improvement. We had a data system that everyone could put into so you then had a big picture of the school and so individual needs of schools were known and where the issues were. We used the council's auditing facilities as well – it was a matter of putting all this information together and getting a big picture of each individual school and focusing the support to the needs of that school and not just giving blanket cover.
>
> Peter Passam: Governor of the Best Start Federation; the strategic management board of the federated PRU & non-executive director The Learning Trust

The capacity within the borough has also been increased by professional collaboration.[60] One example is through the development of school federations. Within a federation each school has its own head of school with an Executive Head who leads the federation. The federations enable staff to work closely with colleagues in other schools within their federation.

[60]Collaboration is dealt with in more depth in another section of this report; see contents for page reference.

It has become an effective way to share best practice and has helped raise the standard of teaching and learning quickly and efficiently. Federations in Hackney developed by linking a failing school with a strong one. The strategy developed as it went along and it is covered more in the Collaboration section.

> Clear definition of a failing school is failing leadership, it has to start at the top. It's always about the leadership and the professional development of staff. Nine out of ten times it's headteachers who have been there twenty or thirty years – stuck in their ways, who don't like change and who have got away with it. In the past there wasn't enough stringent monitoring in place to see the people, they hid below the radar – they coasted – were satisfactory and hit the national averages.
>
> The Learning Trust came along and started looking closer at schools, understanding their problems and trying to find solutions. The problem was when it was leadership the only solution was to put in someone from outside. Consultants are very expensive, so the Learning Trust asked 'what can we do? There has to be better ways of doing this. We have excellent schools within the authority, outstanding and way above outstanding. What can we do to support the other schools?'
>
> Federations – you have an outstanding headteacher who has a very strong vision that can be seen to make a difference, they have a way of bringing the best out of their staff, and they have worked internally and developed strong leadership skills from inside the school.

Peter Passam: Governor of the Best Start Federation; the strategic management board of the federated PRU & non-executive director The Learning Trust

The practice of developing federations is not without criticism. The Learning Trust recognises that it does not suit all schools and also that it does not suit all headteachers. Some heads like to be independent and if they were allied with other schools in a federation they would lose their autonomy. This may encourage them to leave the borough to take up a headship elsewhere which, in turn, would result in the lack of depth because deputies may not want to become heads under these circumstances. It could mean that the Trust would end up spending money on training these heads only for them to put this training into use elsewhere.

> We will always question when a headship come up 'Could this school be linked to another school with an executive principal?' But it isn't our only favoured method. What we've realised is that if we only did federations we would lose the whole layer of investment that we have put into our aspiring leaders programme. They would go off and do a headship in another borough and all that we've invested we lose. And we won't get them back until they're ready to be an executive principal and they might never come back because I don't think everybody can do it. I think it's the top 5 – 10% of heads who can do that role because it's very difficult.
>
> Tricia Okoruwa: Deputy Director The Learning Trust

The Learning Trust did not limit itself to learning from within Hackney. There was a deliberate strategy to offer headteachers opportunities for international study visits to Ontario, Finland and the United States. Internationally renowned educators were invited to conferences in Hackney and leading researchers in the UK worked with schools in Hackney. This enrichment and professional engagement resulted in many innovations adapted from what works well in other countries.

> We've been given access to some of the most forward thinking people who are working internationally. We've had strong links with schools and local authorities in other countries and there's been a real sense of making sure that people get out there and have access to sharp thinking, experiences which challenge our thinking that keep us well and truly informed. It's really leading edge stuff.

Karen Coulthard: Headteacher Berger Primary School

Developing the capacity within Hackney is about developing the relationships between the Trust's officers and the 73 schools within the borough.

> We're learning as we go along. In the last two or three years I've been more explicitly conscious of doing certain things, really looking at developing them. So two or three years ago I thought we can't just be having business meetings all the time, we're going to reserve time to do development by looking at ourselves and our role and how we interface with schools. And that's how we've shaped things much more. We've created materials and toolkits for schools.

> One of the elements of it is the intellectual capacity and we've spent a lot of time looking at research, going to visit people on international studies, we've had these people back, we've challenged them with an international perspective. Most of these headteachers know that they are getting much more that they would get in another local authority. We have put a lot in but we have got a lot out as well. We're putting it in because we know it will pay off.

Tricia Okoruwa: Deputy Director The Learning Trust

The Learning Trust's strategy and its planning can be neatly summed up by the Chief Executive. Note the use of 'we' which again reinforces the team spirit which the Trust has fostered from the start.

> What we built in the first five to six years was sufficient capacity to allow us to work on a broader agenda without taking our eye of the educational ball, so it's been a sign of the success of the Learning Trust from top to bottom.

Alan Wood: Chief Executive The Learning Trust

Challenge

Accept challenges, so that you may feel the exhilaration of victory.
George S. Patton

We have already indicated that support and challenge are both essential for capacity-building. The Learning Trust quickly established a zero tolerance attitude to low expectations. There was a clear refusal to accept poverty (or anything else) as an excuse for low performance by students in GCSE and national tests. On its own, this kind of challenge would soon alienate schools and achieve little in terms of system-wide improvement. Combined with the support we outline in the previous section, we find that The Learning Trust established a compassionate but robust relationship with schools; 'tough love' if you understand that expression. The importance of challenge is equal to that of support. Our findings indicate that without challenge improvements would have been slower, if at all.

When The Learning Trust came into existence one of its first priorities was to challenge the preconceived ideas about the poor educational outcomes of Hackney's children. They set out to convince people that students in Hackney are as capable of achieving as well as students anywhere else. The low preconceptions, which were deeply ingrained within all areas of the community, had resulted from years of an under-performing education service. We asked the Chair of The Learning Trust how did the Trust go about changing the mind-set and convince people that children in Hackney were fully deserving of a good education?

> I think just by ferocious assertion and challenging anyone who felt otherwise. I know that a head was removed having said: "Well what can you expect from children like this?
>
> Richard Hardie: Chair of The Learning Trust

The Chief Executive puts it much more bluntly.

> We dealt very hard with the nonsense.

Alan Wood: Chief Executive The Learning Trust

The Learning Trust was determined to prove that Hackney children were equal to children anywhere else in the country if they were afforded the same chances in their education. The Chief Executive explains the importance of establishing their own credibility first.

> We had a deliberate, focused and very clear strategy. Running through that strategy would be a complete vein of not tolerating low standards. When you're hopeless, when you're useless – to tell people they're not very good is irrelevant. No-one's going to take any notice of you. We ensured our position by improving things and showing we had the capacity and the competence to say what needs to be done. And we made clear we would try to improve things but if it got to the point, in our judgement, where things did not improve we would not sit back; we would act.

Alan Wood: Chief Executive The Learning Trust

The Learning Trust has maintained this focus throughout its ten years and its determination has now been vindicated by the continued upward spiral in its examination results which now see both primary and secondary schools above the national averages

> The Trust has remained true to that focus and that focus is expressed as the moral authority to work with schools - to encourage, to challenge, to work with, to set standards for schools, to model schools and to be the community's voice about the quality of education.

Alan Wood: Chief Executive The Learning Trust

The challenge to improve the quality of Hackney's education provision began with a priority to improve GCSE results in secondary schools. One of the Deputy Directors explains.

> At the beginning the focus was on secondary schools. There was a clear message that failure was not going to be tolerated anymore and that if a school wasn't good enough, all radical and possible solutions would be looked at. Some of the heads felt quite threatened by that. It was very much a top down model, it was autocratic leadership style, directive etc., but that was the right type of leadership for that stage. It had to be quite direct; it had to be clear in establishing what the intention was they were setting out to do. So right in the very beginning for secondary it was clear what the Learning Trust wanted to do. It wanted to make all secondary schools good or better. It was prepared to close them if they weren't; it was also prepared to engage with the academies programme which at the time, politically, not many people were up for. It was very strategic to regenerate secondary education rather than believe in academies, it was a means to an end. It was clear about what was going to happen.

Tricia Okoruwa: Deputy Director The Learning Trust

The Learning Trust did not hesitate to intervene in weak schools; in fact this is one of its key characteristics, the ability to move quickly and effectively when presented with a problem. The fact there was little, if any, political bureaucracy made speedy intervention easy. Because of its high level of involvement with the schools, The Learning Trust was able to identify any problems at an early stage.

> To have a well-managed organisation ready to intervene with weak schools has been of vital importance. The Learning Trust's ability to start to intervene early is what has distinguished it from elsewhere.
>
> Richard Hardie: Chair of The Learning Trust

A headteacher recognises the challenges schools face from The Learning Trust but understands the necessity.

> The Learning Trust is hugely challenging. If you talk to people in other authorities, they don't have that level of intervention. But it's been necessary in Hackney. We couldn't carry on bumbling along the bottom.
>
> Sian Davies: Executive Principal Primary Advantage Federation

The Learning Trust was determined that there was to be no excuses given for the lack of improvement within Hackney schools. It had outlined its raison d'etre from the outset and set the standards for improving the aspirations, outcomes and life chances for Hackney students.

> The Learning Trust has been very good at peeling away excuses to get down to actuality – school leadership and systems in the school – that we need to address. It's not about anything other than 'What are you doing with these children in your school?'
>
> Alan Wood: Chief Executive The Learning Trust

If schools remained persistent in their excuses as to why the students in their school were underachieving, The Learning Trust would have the definitive answer.

> You can challenge a school on its performance –
> the head may say 'Look at my intake, look at my
> SEN and our numbers of children on free school
> meals' and you can say 'Look at the school next
> door to you who have exactly the same intake and
> how well they're doing.' You just can't sit back and
> allow excuses to shape the way you think about
> what your children can achieve.

Elaine Peers: Head of partnerships and safeguarding, former
head of school place planning The Learning Trust

The high expectations by The Learning Trust that all
schools would engage with the raising of educational
standards and improve the quality of teaching and
learning within the borough was maintained by the
rigorous way that the Trust monitored the schools.

> There's been a rigour that's been brought in.
> There's an expectation that you absolutely have
> to improve and I would say that everyone's
> been involved in thinking about improvements.
> Some headteachers have been quite resistant
> to it. Because I've been around a long time, I've
> known them for a long time and some people
> who effectively did their own thing suddenly were
> coming under a much more consistent rigour.
> You weren't allowed to get away with doing your
> own thing. There will always be some charismatic
> headteachers and while I sometimes see that as a
> good thing, other times things get lost and rigour
> disappears because of their charisma. I've seen
> those headteachers trained and coaxed to come
> back into core thinking and be more collegiate.

Lizzie Yauner: Head of inclusion team The Learning Trust

Although The Learning Trust has challenged schools
to improve, they have not left the schools to struggle

on their own. One important feature of the Trust is that it is a team working together to improve Hackney's education. The head of Governors' Support explains:

> If a school is in difficulty The Learning Trust are there like a ton of bricks. Everybody is down there to sort them out. They're not telling them what to do, but helping them. If someone isn't up to the job, they're quickly told 'You're not up to the job. Just be modest and move on.'

Michael McCabe: Governor Services Officer The Learning Trust

A primary headteacher appreciates this support and contrasts it with what happened before The Learning Trust was established.

> I remember when we had really poor SATs results in 2002. We had the results in July and the following May someone came into school to ask me about the previous results. But prior to that we knew it was a difficult and demanding year group. I tried to speak to everyone about what was actually going on and no-one came in. Now if I emailed (the Deputy Director) and asked for help, you'd get the squad in. You feel now you have a meaningful conversation if things are not on track and there is support. It's a really good dialogue, you don't feel inspected.

Karen Coulthard: Headteacher Berger Primary School

The improvement in educational standards resulting from schools in Hackney rising to the challenge set by the Learning Trust has developed an element of competition within the borough. While the schools collaborate and help each other, there is also a friendly rivalry which encourages good schools to outdo each other.

> I think there's a level of healthy competition now where you've got lots more good schools who will bump each other up. It's like having one or two good teachers, it lifts the whole thing. It's not about one or two good schools that have been good for years. It's not like that anymore. There are good schools all over the place, in the most challenging bits of the borough.

Sian Davies: Executive Principal Primary Advantage Federation

Today, it is not just the Learning Trust which has high expectations in Hackney. The stakeholders in the borough now have a changed perception, brought about by the rising trend in results that Hackney has achieved since 2002.

> I go back to when we were in the Council and Ofsted first started coming in to inspect the nurseries. People were happy when they got satisfactory. The thought at that time of Ofsted coming in was really daunting. I think we are a lot further now and the aim is to get a 'Good' outcome at least, although the aspiration is for 'Outstanding'. There are still some providers that haven't reached that level yet but the overall expectation has changed. But not just our expectation at theTrust, I'm talking about expectations among the maintained, voluntary and private sectors as well.

Ann Seago: Senior Family Information Officer The Learning Trust

Challenges by The Learning Trust are not only for schools. The Trust's own leaders are subject to the same robust approach when things don't go as well as the Board expects. The Deputy Director recalls how that felt.

> 66 That was a painful learning experience. It didn't surprise me we dipped by 1% because we had gone up 7% the year before.[61] It was no shock to go down and it was not statistically significant. But the actual response to going down, internally, was quite challenging. But it played in my favour because I hate not doing something well, so it made me think 'Right, that's it. I'm going to show you', even though at the time it was hard to take. 99

Tricia Okoruwa: Deputy Director The Learning Trust

The challenges made by The Learning Trust are not seen as one-way traffic. Staff within the Trust feel safe and valued enough to be able to challenge what the Trust leadership is asking of them and this has helped the feeling of 'togetherness' which encompasses the whole of education within Hackney.

> 66 It is easy to challenge here as well. You will be listened to. I could go and talk to Steve Belk (Director) and he will listen to me. I can go and sit with Alan (Chief Executive) or Tricia (Deputy Director). They're not people you don't talk to as you walk past. That's what is nice about it; you can say 'Hmmm I'm not too sure about that.' I do feel that we're made to feel confident enough to challenge in a positive light. 99

Ann Seago: Senior Family Information Officer The Learning Trust

As well as whole school intervention by the Trust, the quality of teaching provision within the borough came under scrutiny and became one of the main areas targeted for improvement. The Deputy Director spells out the Trust's typical challenging approach.

[61] In 2009 the national test results for eleven year-olds in Hackney fell by 1%.

> We've said to schools that 80% of teaching should be good or better and you can get there within a year. Some of them (teachers) are horrified, but a lot of them have done it so we're sticking hard with that message now.

Tricia Okoruwa: Deputy Director The Learning Trust

The levels and importance of expected quality of teaching has become even more apparent within the federations of schools. The Chair of Governors of one federation describes how they approach teachers when they come into the federation.

> Satisfactory teaching isn't good enough especially in Hackney. Satisfactory teaching is not acceptable and we make that clear when we go into a new school (joining the federation). At the first meeting when we talk about federations and supporting schools we'll sit there and say 'If you're not a good teacher we'll help you to become good and better. But if you don't think you're capable of becoming a good teacher you might want to consider whether you want to work for us or not because we don't accept anything other than good teaching. If you're only satisfactory you will be put on a support plan. If within a certain time you don't improve, you may need to consider your future elsewhere.'

Peter Passam: Governor of the Best Start Federation; the strategic management board of the federated PRU & non-executive director The Learning Trust

Teaching across Hackney has improved. It may not all be good yet but the significant improvements so far are revealed by the GCSE and national test scores and confirmed by headteachers.

66 Teaching has got better; it was another of the expectations. As a school you wanted them (students) to have better schools, better teaching, better resources , a better environment because as a school you're expecting of them, they will expect of you. 99

Cheryl Day: Headteacher Clapton Girls' Technology College

This challenging approach by The Learning Trust is a crucial aspect to capacity building. It has resulted in a change in the perception of what children can achieve in Hackney. Poverty is no longer accepted as a reason for under-achievement. Expectations continue to rise, just like the test scores.

66 There are lots of things that have contributed to the improvement in Hackney schools. One of them is aspiration. I think people's heads have lifted and we've looked around and seen that we can do better for children in Hackney. 99

Sian Davies: Executive Principal Primary Advantage Federation

We considered earlier that pressure and support are the yin and yang of capacity building in schools. The importance of this philosophy is harmony and our study indicates that is the key to success for systemic improvement. As long as challenge is in harmony with support then system improvements are rapid as we have seen in Hackney. The crucial lesson here is that challenge and support are balanced in equilibrium. If the balance shifts too far in either direction, it won't work.

Courage

Courage is going from failure to failure without losing enthusiasm.   Winston Churchill

We learn how The Learning Trust displayed remarkable courage. It never avoided making difficult decisions and acting on them quickly. It was always prepared to be unpopular if that was necessary in order to achieve their moral purpose – what is best for students in Hackney. It was always prepared to act responsibly on their behalf.

> Decisions were taken quickly to close failing secondary schools, to intervene where there has been weak leadership, to experiment for example with federations... to have noticed smartly that if you wanted to have priority for capital expenditure you had to get in the Academies programme.

Richard Hardie: Chair of The Learning Trust

Before exploring the ways that The Learning Trust showed courageous leadership, we draw attention to a condition that complements courage and enabled swift action. As a private company, The Learning Trust is responsible to its board. There are no lengthy, drawn-out political processes requiring consultations before decisions are taken. In the past Hackney Council, like others in England, was paralysed by its democratic processes to the extent that any decision, let alone a controversial one, was impossible. Even in well-run local authorities, these decision-making procedures hamper decisive action. In 2002, the community in Hackney deserved more than that when The Learning Trust stepped in.

> The Trust is characterised by that fleet-footedness and its ability to move quickly.

Paul Adnitt: Former Head of Performance and Equalities The Learning Trust

Fortunately The Learning Trust did not allow itself to be bogged down by time-wasting procedures. The situation was carefully analysed by people with expertise in school improvement, rather than politicians without such deep understanding, and controversial decisions were made followed by swift, crucial action.

> It's not about taking the politics out of it but as a stand-alone body the Trust can be perhaps bolder in terms of action. They would take the flak over the removal of heads, or the removal of a governing body, or whatever it may be. The ability to step in without any political overlay has been helpful.

Tricia Okoruwa: Deputy Director The Learning Trust

Officers in the Trust whose responsibility it was to monitor the schools needed courage to look at the data on the schools, see where improvements needed to be made and face reality. It became obvious that schools had been allowed to deteriorate and would continue in that vein if remedial action was not taken quickly. It was apparent that there were more schools in serious difficulty than previously thought. This was the consequence of years of fire-fighting and helping schools to limp through Ofsted inspections and then moving on to the next school, rather than tackling the underlying problems. The Deputy Director tells us how she needed courage to speak the truth.

(After a term in post talking to the Director)

> I had to tell him. 'I'm not really sure whether to share this with you. You know there are about eight schools in a category.[62] Well after looking at all the schools' data and talking to officers working with the schools, you've got the same number again at risk.' What I wasn't prepared to do was to put

[62] The outcome of an unsatisfactory Ofsted inspection is when the school is placed 'in a category'. There are two categories: schools that fail the inspection require 'special measures' and schools with serious weaknesses are given a 'notice to improve'. School in both categories are monitored by Ofsted until they improve.

sticking plasters on these schools anymore
and that's what had been done. All of these
schools should have been in categories years ago.
Before an Ofsted inspection that's what had been
done – they had put sticking plasters on,
got them through the inspection and then after
walked away. It became a cycle. I knew that wasn't
what we should do. I also knew I had to do two
things, – I had to do the fire fighting and I had
to do the school improvement at the same time.
It wasn't one or the other.

Tricia Okoruwa: Deputy Director The Learning Trust

It was at this point that the Learning Trust really started
to earn their reputation that low standards and excuses
were not acceptable. They began to look beyond the
fact that a headteacher was a nice, well-meaning
person with their own personal responsibilities and
livelihood to think about. They recognised that one
person could not be allowed to have an adverse effect
on the learning outcomes and therefore future of a
whole school. This was when they had to make really
difficult, soul-searching decisions about the staff
that were running schools. The Trust had the moral
obligation to ensure that all Hackney children were
receiving a good, if not better, standard of education.
A headteacher testifies to this reality.

It is brutal and it is harsh. People are upset; it's
their mortgage, their family and their livelihood.
But then it's also 230 children's futures and lives
that are at risk. Somebody somewhere has got
to make that decision as to where that balance
lies. And if the governing body won't do it and the
headteacher doesn't do it, then somebody has
got to because it's children's futures which are
at stake.

Sian Davies: Executive Principal Primary Advantage Federation

The Chief Executive acknowledges that The Learning Trust had the courage to face that reality.

> There was a view that primary schools in Hackney were basically OK. There was a small layer of good primaries and a whole layer of those muddling-along schools and then a very small number of year-after-years, badly performing schools. The culture of primary heads was defensive, inward-looking and protective. The primary strategy was that the primaries which were in special measures – there were thirteen – we got them out but it went wrong and one or two of them went back in. So we did something which I think is characteristic. We removed the senior staff who were responsible for those failures. We can't tolerate failure.

Alan Wood: Chief Executive The Learning Trust

Of course removing the senior staff responsible does not improve a school. It may prevent further damage but the improvement only begins when a good leader is appointed to the school. Finding good leaders is difficult enough, attracting them to Hackney at the time was a bigger challenge. This was a known danger and for this reason we recognise the courageous actions of staff in The Learning Trust. The reputation of Hackney, its education and its schools, was such that it was unable to attract good quality staff. Schools were also unable to retain teachers so turnover was huge. The Learning Trust wanted to stop this. They knew they had to change from the top down. They weeded out the poor quality headteachers even though they may have found themselves in a difficult situation. They were determined to get rid of poor quality staff rather than tolerate them. The Deputy Director admits that these were difficult decisions and reveals her guiding philosophy.

> ❝ Nobody wanted to come and work in Hackney so
> initially you thought 'Well do we get rid of these
> heads or not?' And then we said 'Well you know
> what...' I only went with the philosophy I used in
> schools where I would never have an inadequate
> teacher and I always found a better one. So I found
> the same strategy worked. If you always hang on
> and say 'Well there's nobody better out there'
> then you'll never improve the system. It was a big
> gamble; we moved on so many headteachers that
> we could have ended up in a worse situation. ❞
>
> Tricia Okoruwa: Deputy Director The Learning Trust

It was not just in schools where ineffective staff were
moved on. The same approach was used within the
organisation itself. A secondary headteacher recalls the
turnover of officers.

> ❝ The Learning Trust was characterised by the
> fact that if you weren't good enough, you went.
> The number of staff who were sacked was
> phenomenal. In a way, for whatever reason, you
> just saw this massive turnover of officers all the
> time. However, there are some key officers who are
> still here today. ❞
>
> Jenny Wilkins: Principal Skinners' Academy

If the problem was more deeply-rooted than the
leadership of the school then the Trust had even more
courageous decisions to take. It is tough enough to
remove individual staff who are not up to scratch but
when a change of personnel at the top is not enough
to turn a school around then closing the school needs
to be considered. Again we find The Learning Trust
was prepared to say 'enough is enough' and close
the school. They may have been afraid of community
unease at the thought of closing a school and that is
why it calls for courage. It was part of the bigger picture

to be able to say to Hackney residents - this school has been in special measures for years there is nothing more to be done. We need to close it and start afresh. Mike Tomlinson recalls these decisions.

> We (the Learning Trust) intervened strongly and in two cases closed the schools. With the first school (Kingsland) we were told categorically by the Council that the school would not be closed as they had tried before and had had to call the Police in to remove people from the Town Hall because of the riot. I said 'I hear you – but watch me, I'm going to close it.' And it closed.

Sir Mike Tomlinson: first Chair of The Learning Trust

When schools started to be closed the local community began to take on board the message that the Trust was really serious about improving the standard of education. It was very important that that was the message which got out into the borough. The departure of headteachers and other staff and the closure of continually failing schools was a good indicator of The Learning Trust's courage and determination.

> There was the insistence that kids could do well in Hackney schools and we needed to persuade everyone, slowly but surely, to take a chance. I think that they (the schools) thought we were a much more coherent body that they had seen before. We were doing things like closing schools; headteachers were disappearing.

Alan Wood: Chief Executive The Learning Trust

While it was difficult to attract good headteachers to replace those that were removed, building new schools to replace those that were closed was an even bigger challenge. When the Trust first considered how to improve education in Hackney the strategy was to close poor schools and create brand new ones. This immediately removed the baggage from the past which was associated with the old schools. New secondary schools would be more attractive, have better facilities and be better fit for purpose. They would start with a single intake into Year 7 and grow naturally year on year. The new schools would be able to create their own identities and instil their own ethos right from day one.

> The policy of closing failing schools and creating new schools from scratch was a good one.
>
> Steve Belk: Director of Learning and Standards The Learning Trust

This would cost a lot of money which the Trust did not have. True to form The Learning Trust had already identified the only area of Government funding which they could access to build these new schools – the Academies Programme. This was political dynamite. Two miles down the road, at Islington Green, all hell was let loose when the Council consulted the community about building a new academy. A massive opposition campaign was led by the teacher unions. The furore and adverse publicity caused the original sponsors to pull out. Every obstacle that could be found was used to delay the project by at least three years.

Once more we find The Learning Trust taking a courageous decision. Whilst other local authorities were looking at perhaps one or two of the academies the Trust was looking at potentially five. What the Trust did though, was to stipulate conditions for anyone sponsoring an academy. This ensured they were being built for the good of Hackney residents, not just for the benefit of the sponsors. A secondary headteacher acknowledges the courage needed to open academies in Hackney.

> " I've always said it was a very brave move to have academies in Hackney at the time. But actually something needed to be done that was quite radical. Most local authorities wouldn't take on a lot of academies because they don't control them anymore. I thought it was a move that indicated we're here to raise standards as our first priority. We want to give people in Hackney the very best that we can. "
>
> Jenny Wilkins: Principal Skinners' Academy

With the moral compass of improving Hackney's education leading the way, The Learning Trust is always prepared to be innovative in how it achieves its goals. The Trust has never been daunted by the prospect of removing poor quality staff and the repercussions which that may have entailed. It looked at itself, cut out any dead wood and had the courage to set the most ambitious goals. Having kept its eye fully focused on those goals, the Learning Trust has achieved above and beyond expectations.

We began by describing courage as a character trait that drives people into dangerous situations. Finding yourself in a dangerous situation that may be due to circumstances beyond your control does not call for courage. We end this section by considering what motivates people in The Learning Trust to be courageous? Why is it that they will overcome their fears and choose the options that others would avoid? We suggest they are compelled by the inspirational dream – in this case to make Hackney schools so good that parents will struggle to get their children admitted.

Creativity

The problem is never how to get new, innovative thoughts into your mind, but how to get old ones out. Every mind is a building filled with archaic furniture. Clean out a corner of your mind and creativity will instantly fill it.

Dee Hock

Creativity is an essential ingredient for capacity-building. Improvements cannot be secured simply by continuing to do what you have already done before. The Learning Trust knew from the outset that it needed to stimulate innovation and change. We learn how the Trust enjoyed its freedom from political constraints to experiment widely. Autonomy was devolved throughout the organisation and we learn how officers were empowered to adapt national strategies as they felt appropriate. New campaigns were created in partnerships with voluntary and private sector organisations. The Learning Trust was able to use its funding flexibly for maximum benefit and it was in the vanguard for Government funding initiatives, never missing an opportunity to improve facilities for education in Hackney.

The Learning Trust was independent of Hackney Council and therefore had its own identity. This enabled the Trust to formulate its own code of practice. Working within its remit to improve education and the future prospects and life chances of Hackney's young people, the Trust was able to make things happen quickly without having to be sanctioned by the Council after numerous committee and council meetings.

[63] Paul worked with the LEA intervention team at the Department for Education and Skills when The Learning Trust was established. He is referring to the specific context of Hackney in 2002.

66 We needed something more radical that really removed the running of education from the political sphere in a way which had never been done before.[63] 99

Paul Adnitt: Former Head of Performance and Equalities The Learning Trust

> 66 Although there is a process of continuing scrutiny by the council the fact that we are independent and able in some ways to be experimental without seeking permission, or without testing the political water has allowed us to be innovative but also to move quickly, even at the risk of public controversy. But the guiding principle has always been 'What's the right thing for the outcomes of young people?' 99

Richard Hardie: Chair of The Learning Trust

People working in the Trust were empowered and encouraged to be creative. Mike Tomlinson explains how they started it.

> 66 We simply said 'We're here, we've got every bit of support you want, just tell us.' I said to the Learning Trust people that I didn't want any bureaucracy; I don't want any multiple form-filling to get something done. Make a damn decision – get on with it. I don't want reams of paper going around. 99

Sir Mike Tomlinson: first Chair of The Learning Trust

The same approach was taken with schools that were doing well. The Chief Executive makes this point.

> 66 There was a saying encapsulated by one of the heads who said 'The schools that do well in Hackney do well despite Hackney education.' So we decided that wasn't what The Learning Trust was about – our job is not to get in the way but to take things out of the way. 99

Alan Wood: Chief Executive The Learning Trust

A primary headteacher acknowledges this and relates the innovation encouraged by the Trust as one of the factors that have improved test scores over the last ten years.

> For me, it's very much about the innovation and creativity that have been sparked through the mechanisms the Learning Trust has put in place.

Sian Davies: Executive Principal Primary Advantage Federation

The fact that the Trust was responsible for itself along with the freedom the Trust had and its willingness to listen, meant that it began to attract innovative and creative professionals. Just the kind that The Learning Trust needed. The Chair explains.

> The distinctive characteristic of being independent of the Council and of being prepared to try things has attracted increasingly talented applicants to teach in the schools and within the Learning Trust itself. It's much easier to attract people if there is a ten year career to offer.

Richard Hardie: Chair of The Learning Trust

The Learning Trust stimulated creativity in two ways. First by empowering its workforce and encouraging them to be innovative. Second by listening to everyone's views, particularly when they are critical, so that they learn new ideas and different ways of thinking.

> The Trust has just given people that ability. They have empowered stakeholders, they've given parents the voice, they've given headteachers and governors the voice and they really do listen.

Peter Passam: Governor of the Best Start Federation;
the strategic management board of the federated PRU &
non-executive director The Learning Trust

This degree of autonomy has allowed The Learning Trust and schools in Hackney to look at their working practices and see where they could reshape how things were done. Although there were obvious constraints that the schools had to follow the national curriculum, the Trust encouraged people to adapt other areas to suit their needs, rather than blindly following national strategies or implementing policy directives without question. Here we have two examples – one from primary and the other from secondary schools.

> I think it's important how we've shaped things to suit our own purposes. Take the national strategy for School Improvement Partners. When that came in we already had our own programme where schools had a core of so many days support in a year. And we have changed and developed that consistently. One of the key breakthroughs for me, which if I'd been more confident or knowledgeable earlier on, I would have broken with the national strategies earlier. What they had done initially had been of use but what they were offering beyond that would not take us any further. The year that we dipped, I thought 'You know what, if we're going to get beaten up for this then I'm going to do it my way.' And we didn't engage with the national strategies at all that year. Some of the national strategy materials are pitched at the wrong stage of development for some of our schools. We had a much greater understanding of school improvement, teaching and learning and decided to do less rather than try and please everybody. So we focused on leadership by growing good leaders and developing the leaders we've got and then improving our level of teaching and learning.

Tricia Okoruwa: Deputy Director The Learning Trust

> A lot of the guidance we received was from the secondary national strategy and they gave us scripts like you must do x, y and z. In some cases I thought 'This actually doesn't reflect what we should be doing with the schools.' But because

there was accountability to them we did. However
I think that over the years, because we had a
better sense of the local needs as opposed to the
national needs, we were able to tailor it. 99

Bukky Yusuf: Senior science consultant The Learning Trust

The freedom to be creative and come up with borough-
wide initiatives has also proven to have a positive long
term effect on the success of education in Hackney.
One example is the Words Unite – Get Hackney Reading
campaign which was launched in 2008 and which was
aimed at everyone in Hackney. To be able to involve the
whole of a multi-ethnic and culturally diverse borough
through workshops, homework clubs, targeted reading
groups, storytelling using local libraries and reading
challenges was a unique initiative.

66 Get Hackney Reading was one of the things
I'm most proud about. To engage the whole
community in getting Hackney reading. They really
did champion it with the help of the voluntary
sector. It is obvious when you look at the data, we
tracked it back in 2010 from the GCSE results and
it made a significant difference whether you got a
2b or a 2c in reading at age 7. We had to convince
people and we will probably have to do it again
because of funding cuts, and convince schools
to focus on reading up to age 7. Get them reading
before they go on to key stage 2. 99

Tricia Okoruwa: Deputy Director The Learning Trust

Creativity was not only limited to making changes to
the curriculum or being able to do things at speed. The
Learning Trust was fully responsible for its own budget
and could decide for itself how it spent its money. The
Trust was sure that the budget made available for the
year was theirs to spend on education and they were
safe in the knowledge that any surplus would not be

clawed back by the Council to be spent elsewhere. This meant that they were able to be creative as to how, when and where they spent their money.

At the inception of the Learning Trust one of the things Mike Tomlinson insisted he wanted for Hackney was a high quality professional development centre as the existing one was in a poor state of repair. Referring to the existing teacher's centre, Mike Tomlinson tells us.

> I said 'One of the first things I want is a new teacher's CPD centre. You cannot put people in there and have them (teachers) believe you're seriously concerned about their development and their well-being.'
>
> Sir Mike Tomlinson: first Chair of The Learning Trust

The Learning Trust was able to achieve this goal by good husbandry and without it having an adverse effect on other areas of education. The Chief Executive explains how it was done.

> What we have been good at is making the money more effective. We did strip out lots of jobs, unnecessary layers. We did strip out a lot of inefficient people. We were able to make much better use of money including finding sufficient funds to spend £4,500,000 on the Tomlinson Centre, which wasn't a burden on the Council and they get it back at the end of 10 years.
>
> Alan Wood: Chief Executive The Learning Trust

The purpose of the Learning Trust was to transform education within Hackney and in order to do this the Trust knew that it would have to build new secondary schools if it was to persuade more parents to choose a Hackney school. At the time the Learning Trust took over in 2002 only 40% of parents opted to send their

children to a Hackney secondary school. Although
the Trust had responsibility for its budget and the
Academies programme was in full swing, the Trust still
needed to obtain extra funding to improve and update
the existing schools. The members of the Board were
adept at keeping their fingers on the pulse and making
sure they were completely up to date with any initiatives
whereby monies were made available. Thus when the
Building Schools for the Future (BSF) programme was
introduced in 2005 The Learning Trust got its bid in and
secured over £170 million from the DfES with which
to transform or rebuild the existing Hackney schools
to bring them all into the 21st Century. The building
works are staggered, but all Hackney schools should
be transformed by the Autumn of 2014. This creativity
again allows all of Hackney's residents to be involved
through planning and creating the educational vision
for their schools and also creates places which the local
community can use.

> The Learning Trust got its act together on BSF
> and Hackney was in there. They knew that the
> academies had brand new things and the existing
> schools were in dilapidated, looked after, but
> dilapidated buildings. So they got the bid in, they
> kept their eye on what was available. There was
> lots of investment in Hackney.
>
> Cheryl Day: Headteacher Clapton Girls' Technology College

The academies programme has also been a major factor
in the success of the Trust in raising the expectation and
aspiration of Hackney children. The insistence by the
Trust that any potential sponsors had to meet specific
criteria was a very creative and forward-thinking move
as it ensured that the best interests of Hackney were at
the centre of the regeneration of the schools. One of the
specific requirements was that the academies had to be
a start-up school from Year 7 rather than there simply

be a close down, with a change of name and uniform. This meant that the ethos of the new school could be set from day one rather than there be the constant battle with the legacy of the old school.

> It was very smart of the Learning Trust to insist that all academies had to be start - up schools. Most of the problems have been with conversion academies. If you start a school from scratch you have this amazing advantage that your board of governors share one common purpose.
>
> Richard Hardie: Chair of The Learning Trust

The Learning Trust also did not hesitate when trying to be creative about how it could share excellent practice between schools. Hackney has embraced the world of both 'clusters' and 'networks' of schools whereby information and expertise is shared. It has also has taken the idea a step further to form federations of primary schools. This again encourages creativity in that staff can be swapped between schools as and when needed, especially where it contributes to raising the bar with regard to teaching and learning.

Encouraging creativity means encouraging people to take risks. If no risks are taken then there will never be any new ideas developed. For risk-taking and creativity to be effective, staff must feel secure if things don't work out from time to time. If The Learning Trust experienced difficulties when it first experimented with federations it did not allow this to deter it from trying something which it knew would improve Hackneys education. We end this section with an example of risk- taking that didn't work out as it was intended to. However, this experience has not diminished creativity at all. As Richard Farson maintains, if you don't fail at something it generally means that you're not trying hard enough.[64]

[64]Farson, R. *The Case for Failure* in Blankstein, Cole & Houston (2007) Engaging Every Learner. Thousand Oaks: Corwin

" We don't like to stop there, we like to experiment.
We looked at the model and the next one we made
a mistake with really. It was a mismatch. It came
early on before we really knew what we were doing.
It was my lack of understanding about school
improvement that I've got now but didn't have
then, which is around schools at different stages
of development requiring different strategies, or
different partnerships. I went with a head from
an excellent school but she wanted it all to be
organic but the outcomes were not improving. It
was a painful experience for the head. That made
me realise how the headteacher's philosophy of
education should be matched to the situation.
To begin with it (federation policy) was a deficit
model without any doubt. Now we are consulting
on a four school federation and a five school
federation that are about moving from good to
outstanding. "

Tricia Okoruwa: Deputy Director The Learning Trust

Collaboration

Alone we can do so little; together we can do so much.
Helen Keller

There are several dimensions to the way that The
Learning Trust increased capacity in Hackney through
collaboration. We learn how they overcame the
tensions that existed with Hackney Council at the
start of their contract to engage the Council with
their secondary school strategy to build a string
of academies for the benefit of the community. By
establishing clear criteria for sponsors, The Learning
Trust and Hackney Council ensured that the academies
were committed to collaboration with other schools in
Hackney. High profile Board members in The Learning
Trust helped other corporate sponsors in the City to
engage with the Hackney community of schools. In
the primary sector we explore the powerful influence
of collaboration through the formation of federations.
While collaboration is successful across Hackney, we
learn how schools retain a competitive edge which
encourages them to out-perform each other.

In 2002 when the Learning Trust took over the running
of the education services there was no relationship
with Hackney Council. The Council had no choice at the
time and understandably resented the Government
intervention. We find that the collaboration between
Hackney Council and The Learning Trust has made a
massive contribution to the turnaround in education.

Over a period of time the relationship between the
Council and Trust improved as the Trust managed
to move education forward. The Council could see
that the Trust had a good focus and began to work
in partnership where they could, especially on the
development and improvement of new and existing
schools in the borough. In reality, they had to work in

partnership as the Council owned the land on which the Trust wanted to build new schools. This working together helped to change the perception that the Trust was working against the Council and led to a more trusting and confident relationship between the two. The Chief Executive of Hackney Council picks up the story from the outset.

> We were in a position in the beginning where we had negotiated a contract. The Council were in a position of wanting to manage that contract to the letter because there were obvious tensions. What happened over a period of years is we gradually moved to a position where we were not so reliant on the contract and were much more reliant on relationships. That was very much helped by the joint working on things like Building Schools for the Future and academies.
>
> We've been heavily involved in the delivery of them. Physically delivering which we've facilitated. I was project sponsor for academies so I've been there making sure buildings are getting done on time, the Council shifting all of the issues it needs to shift to get them done on time. It's been difficult but as Chief Executive I've taken it on and cleared the obstacles which were critical to success.

Tim Shields: Chief Executive Hackney Council

The Chair of The Learning Trust gives us an insight into how relationships were developed.

> There were some tensions at the outset as the Council learned to live with something it couldn't control at a time when the Council itself grew rapidly away from the low point it had reached, also in 2002. Several things prevented that from becoming a clash. One was the sheer ability of the people who were operating in The Learning Trust,

who understood sensitivities but knew what
they were supposed to be doing and knew how
to do it. 🙶

Richard Hardie: Chair of The Learning Trust

We now consider collaboration between the schools
themselves. In order to increase capacity, the Trust
wanted the schools to work together and not as
separate entities. This message went out to the Heads
so that they were aware that it was a team effort by
all involved in education within Hackney and that it
required a collaborative effort to raise the standard
of education provision across the borough. Mike
Tomlinson re-iterates that clear message.

🙶 The Trust told the headteachers that they had
to work to the common good: 'OK, so you're
head of one school but you have a collective
responsibility for every young person in Hackney.
Therefore don't simply send all your difficult pupils
to one school'. 🙶

Sir Mike Tomlinson: first Chair of The Learning Trust

[65]The Academies
programme is roughly
equivalent to American
Charter schools.
Government stipulated
that each academy
should be sponsored
by a corporate, or an
individual, benefactor.
In the original
programme sponsors
had to contribute 10% of
the capital expenditure,
in cash or kind, to
the construction of
the new building.
Once constructed,
the sponsors own
the building and
Government pays all
revenue costs directly
to the academy which
is independent of the
local authority.

The Learning Trust was very specific about how it was
going to manage the introduction of academies into
the borough. It knew that working with Government to
introduce academies was the only way it could finance
brand new schools and transform the life chances of
Hackney residents by providing genuine choice across
a range of excellent secondary schools. Everything
the Learning Trust did was to improve education and
raise the expectations of those living in the borough.
The key to the academy programme in Hackney was
that The Learning Trust and Hackney Council worked in
partnership to choose sponsors who were committed to
Hackney and to working in collaboration.[65]

> We had a very clear and agreed strategy with the council that we wanted there to be a local connection and we wanted a commitment to work in a partnership with other schools so that academies weren't seen as sitting outside on their own. We had a very clear strategy about our expectations of the sponsors and we weren't prepared to say we'll take what you have.

Elaine Peers: Head of partnerships and safeguarding, former head of school place planning The Learning Trust

The criteria for sponsoring an academy in Hackney were made explicit. At its heart was the fact that the sponsor had to have a previous connection with Hackney and therefore understood what was needed and what would work. One of the sponsors confirms from their point of view.

> As the sponsor for an academy we were told that we had to provide a non- denominational, mixed secondary school. Hackney council had the land and the Learning Trust had the veto on the appointment of the sponsors so it was dealing with both of them together. We had to agree on a system of fair banding for admissions, no selection of any kind, even on the specialisms.[66]

Richard Hardie: Chair of The Learning Trust

[66]Specialist schools in England are similar to American magnet schools. Secondary schools need to apply and meet certain criteria to be awarded specialist status such as languages, science, business, sport, performing arts etc. Specialist schools may select up to 10% of their intake according to students' aptitudes.

There are now five academies in Hackney and four faith schools (Christian and Jewish). The non- religious schools are oversubscribed. Parents know that the secular secondary schools provide an excellent education and so do not suddenly start to attend church as their children approach the transfer to secondary school. The Learning Trust's action to transform secondary school provision in Hackney has obviously paid off. Most parents want to send their children to Hackney schools; in fact parents of children in neighboring boroughs also want to have their children educated in Hackney. This is a far cry from the days when parents were voting with their feet to get their children educated out of the borough.

One of the Government's key aims in 2002 was to raise educational standards by encouraging schools to work together to share ideas and good practice. This could involve work on the curriculum but it might also include sharing and leadership across a number of schools. The Education Act 2002 allowed schools to federate or collaborate from September 2003 onwards. The introduction of primary school federations in Hackney is quite unique and it happened early in the history of The Learning Trust. Although there had been cooperation between schools to help each other when in crisis, federations were not part of the Trust's original plan. However, their development and success is down to people in the Trust working collaboratively with headteachers and governing bodies for the wider benefit of students in Hackney. As with all successful innovation, there was initial scepticism and things were worked out gradually as The Learning Trust adapted to changing situations. The Deputy Director responsible for the strategic development of federations in Hackney explains.

" Steve Belk (Director of Standards) brought that idea in. I was quite sceptical at the time. I thought of one headteacher for one school and all that stuff. Over 2003–2004 some deputies came out of one school to work with another in crisis but it wasn't part of a structural organisational change. "
Tricia Okoruwa: Deputy Director The Learning Trust

In 2004 there was a crisis at Holy Trinity Primary School. Standards had dropped the headteacher left and there was insufficient leadership in the school to make the necessary improvements. The Deputy Director of the Trust approached the head of St John and St James Primary school to be Executive Principal of a federation existing of her school with Holy Trinity. St John and St James is an outstanding 'fresh start' school which had been transformed by the current headteacher from the remains of a previous school in the same buildings, with the same children, which had languished in special measures for five years when Hackney Council was in charge of the schools.

> Sian (headteacher of St John & St James) said 'Yes' without having to think twice. She didn't want to sit and meet for five hours to talk about what's and wherewithal's, she just said 'Yes'. Basically we developed the whole model of it as we went along. We didn't know how we were going to do it; we just said yes we'll try. We didn't know what the model would be or what it would look like.
>
> Tricia Okoruwa: Deputy Director The Learning Trust

The development of federations in Hackney has been a response to utilise the capacity of its outstanding schools for a greater benefit. Their development was unplanned to the extent that nobody was planning on schools requiring special measures or developing serious weaknesses. However, the joining together of schools into federations has had to be negotiated carefully and with considerable planning. The Trust has put a great deal of faith into which schools form the federations and the leadership of the Executive Principals. Although federated, each school retains its own identity and is led by a head of school. The advantages of this approach to schools in crisis are clear. The response is rapid, direct and it immediately increases the capacity of the failing school. Within the Hackney federations, each failing school has rapidly improved and they are soon recognised by Ofsted as outstanding schools.

> When an urgent response is required we've been able to respond to that need quite quickly. Although it may be ad hoc in timing, a great deal of strategic thought had been put into at the Learning Trust about whom to approach because they don't want to put another school at risk.
>
> Sian Davies: Executive Principal Primary Advantage Federation

The role of the Executive Principal in these circumstances is challenging. When they bring a weak school into the federation, they have to be diplomatic yet forceful, be good communicators and be forward thinking. Matching schools with people who are going to lead and inspire them to rise to the challenge is different from sending in an advisor or consultant because that's all they do - advise. If the school doesn't want to take the advice then it doesn't have to. Within a federation the relationship is different. The Executive Principal will make sure that what needs to be done is done. That requires tact, diplomacy, integrity and determination. It takes a very skilled person to be able to achieve this without putting everyone's back up. One of the Executive Principals acknowledges this difference.

> Lots of local authority advisers are very skilled at coercing, persuading and encouraging headteachers to do things in certain ways and I have to do that with my heads of school but ultimately the relationship is different.
>
> Sian Davies: Executive Principal Primary Advantage Federation

Collaboration is the essential strategy that makes federations successful. However, it is always a risky endeavour to take another school into the federation. Here again we find that creativity and risk-taking go hand in hand as the Executive Principal points out.

> We always evaluated that risk carefully and I always discuss with the heads of school as my first starting point. If we were to take on another school, can we manage? Do we have the capacity?
>
> Sian Davies: Executive Principal Primary Advantage Federation

The risk is reduced by the strong relationship that exists between the Executive Principals and The Learning Trust. The Principals know that the Trust will back them up fully and provide whatever support the federation needs to ensure success.

> As much as we are in partnership as a group of schools, we also work in partnership with the Learning Trust.
>
> Sian Davies: Executive Principal Primary Advantage Federation

Federations are one way of collaborating but not all heads want to lose their independence. The Learning Trust supports all the schools in Hackney but makes no insistence that a school should become part of a federation or even a network. It's down to each individual head to decide how they want to work rather than the insistence by the Trust that this is how it will be done.

> We've got another situation where the head from a successful school is working with a less successful one. She's taken her deputy with her and the school is very clear they welcome the support but they don't want to be in a federation.
>
> Tricia Okoruwa: Deputy Director The Learning Trust

The Learning Trust has always seen its remit as being part of a team working to improve education in Hackney. This means that when a school is experiencing difficulties the Trust will work with the school to achieve success rather than merely tell it what needs to be done and expect the school to do it. It is all about collaborative working which highlights the fact that this is a partnership. One of the Trust's consultants who works in schools explains.

> Part of the reason for success is the fact that we are prepared to roll up our sleeves and do what has to be done to support the schools whichever way we can. We try to be responsive to schools in terms of what they ask of us so that it's a collaborative approach. We don't go in and tell them what to do; we're actually listening to schools and go in to work alongside them. I think that approach has worked successfully.
>
> Bukky Yusuf: Senior science consultant The Learning Trust

Collaboration has been an important part of the capacity building strategy to transform education in Hackney. The improvements we find in GCSE results and national test scores during The Learning Trust's contract would not have been possible without the successful alliances we have indicated here.

Confidence

*I have not failed 10,000 times. I have successfully found
10,000 ways that will not work.*

Thomas A. Edison

We learn how confidence is essential to success
and well-being. It required inspirational leadership
by The Learning Trust to lift people in Hackney from
the despair they experienced in the years leading up
to the award of the contract in 2002. Confidence in
Hackney schools was at a low point. Parents expressed
concern by moving their children to secondary schools
in neighbouring boroughs; only 40% chose schools
in Hackney. With the Council in the newspaper
headlines for its mismanagement of public services,
crumbling school buildings and schools pilloried for
low standards, you would expect nothing else. We find
self-esteem among the teaching force linked to parents'
confidence in the system. Building parental confidence
and restoring self-esteem became important features
of the work of The Learning Trust. They were achieved
through a combination of inspiration, communication
and celebration which feed off each other.[67]

There was a healthy degree of scepticism in Hackney
when The Learning Trust started. Schools had already
seen one private company, Nord Anglia, come and go
without much noticeable change. While hopes had
risen during Liz Reid's time as director of education, it
was short-lived. Many people were dismayed when she
left suddenly, without explanation.

> Between 1999 and 2000 when Liz Reid was director
> of education there was confidence in her and her
> ability to do it. But the interaction that she often
> shared with the heads around the relationship
> between her and the Council was scary. Heads
> had confidence in Liz Reid and her expertise, the

[67] Communication
and celebration
are important
characteristics. Each is
dealt with in a separate
section. See contents.

problem was those around her; she didn't have many officers and the quality was poor. It wasn't worth having some of them visit you. 🙶

Tricia Okoruwa: Deputy Director The Learning Trust

Once again we find that the appointment of Mike Tomlinson as the Chair of The Learning Trust was a critical factor. Mike quickly breathed inspiration into the organisation and restored hope.

🙶 Getting Mike Tomlinson as Chair was important. He was, and still is, an education statesman. In one stroke he established the credibility of the company. He set the tone from the very beginning that the company was working to raise standards, increase opportunity and to improve well-being and life chances for children in Hackney schools. That was cascaded through senior managers to the whole workforce. 🙶

Neil Weeks: Corporate Governance Officer The Learning Trust

Mike's appointment was a complete surprise to most people within and beyond Hackney.

🙶 They were shocked that someone like Mike Tomlinson would come and work in Hackney. At first there was a conspiracy theory about why the Government sent him in. I think the confidence is in the interface between the schools and The Learning Trust and we worked hard to build that up. 🙶

Tricia Okoruwa: Deputy Director The Learning Trust

As indicated above, confidence was raised through inspiration and celebration which are closely intertwined. However, it was initiated by inspiration and it's not complicated. Mike Tomlinson explains what he did was simple but vital.

> I said to the heads: 'I want this to be the place everyone looks to for educational innovation and improvement. Where people want to come and work because this is the best place to start your career.' The big issue was not to be heavy-handed. I said: 'You can do it. We'll help you do it. We believe in you.' Basically I wanted to raise the self-esteem and confidence of teachers. It was in their boots when we took over. They didn't believe they were good at anything.

Sir Mike Tomlinson: first Chair of The Learning Trust

Everyone we have listened to says the same thing: Mike Tomlinson made an immediate and important positive difference.

> I was there at the first headteachers' conference when Mike Tomlinson spoke to us and it was inspirational. I can remember him walking up and down the corridor talking to us. That had never happened before. No-one had ever talked to us on such a personal level before. That was a huge change. We became people. We felt valued.

Lizzie Yauner: Head of inclusion team The Learning Trust

Of course talk is cheap. Making promises will raise hope but they must be followed by action. Confidence grows only when promises are fulfilled.

> Mike Tomlinson was totally committed to Hackney. He said he would help to get funding and help us to be the best. He went out and said great things about Hackney. When he came we were in an era when the press slammed Hackney and the schools got it because of that. Mike made a significant difference. He did what he said he would. He rolled in resources. He came to meetings and gave us

time. Mike was a confidence builder and we gained confidence in The Learning Trust. 🙿

Cheryl Day: Headteacher Clapton Girls' Technology College

While Mike led by example, confidence building did not rely on his charisma. The Learning Trust deliberately set out to restore people's hope and give them faith that this time things would be different. People in The Learning Trust tell us.

🙿 That was always the big focus – we've got to convince people that this is different and this is going to make a difference. We (The Learning Trust) had to gain the confidence of teachers, headteachers, parents and governors. Building rapport and gaining confidence was a big focus. The way we did it was to ask then what they needed, what had been lacking? And we asked them what we could do for them that would make life easier. 🙿

Peter Passam: Governor of the Best Start Federation; the strategic management board of the federated PRU & non-executive director The Learning Trust

🙿 There was a great emphasis in the beginning of the Trust on repairing relationships which allows you to build a sense of greater aspirations and confidence in those aspirations. Once you set off down that road you start attracting better leaders, attracting better teachers and it builds and builds. 🙿

Paul Adnitt: Former Head of Performance and Equalities The Learning Trust

What began in 2002 as confidence-building grew over the next ten years into the proud, high- performing professional community that exists today. School standards justify this pride and provide evidence of this achievement across Hackney schools together with testimony from many witnesses such as these.

" Within a year people were coming and wanting to know if they could be employed by The Learning Trust whereas before they would want to come and ask how do I get unemployed by Hackney? "

Sir Mike Tomlinson: first Chair of The Learning Trust

" What I believe we (The Learning Trust) have done, apart from anything else, is we've re-created the education community in Hackney. By that I mean the partnership between schools. The pride the teachers and pupils have in schools. But most importantly the pride that the residents of Hackney have for the education service. "

Alan Wood: Chief Executive The Learning Trust

" It's been a joy to work with that team of people. The main thing is the like- mindedness, the passion that Hackney was going to be the best, whether it was Mike Tomlinson or Alan Wood who has seen it all the way through with his team. Through that passion, the consistency of this is the message – whatever we're trying to do is for the benefit of our young people. We want them to have the best opportunities, great resources and make the highest possible achievement. That's been the focus. "

Cheryl Day: Headteacher Clapton Girls' Technology College

" To be the lead in a federation you've got to have a school that's capable of developing leadership and an ethos of collaboration. Within our federation the staff cherish every lesson observation they get because it's done in such a way that supports them and helps them to become outstanding teachers. It gives them confidence. "

Peter Passam: Governor of the Best Start Federation;
the strategic management board of the federated PRU &
non-executive director The Learning Trust

With such increased confidence among parents and in the school workforce across Hackney, it is not surprising that within The Learning Trust there is a highly committed and effective team who gain huge job satisfaction from these outcomes. Everyone we listened to from The Learning Trust enjoys the working culture in the organisation and gave us insights into how The Learning Trust managed to build confidence in Hackney.

> In every workplace you'll get criticisms, some constructive and some otherwise. We organised staff surveys and at first we found people with a gripe always shout loudest. The people who managed the survey say the most important question is 'Would you recommend The Learning Trust as a place to work to other colleagues?' We are getting over 90% responding very positively. There is a culture of autonomy, feeling empowered make decisions and go out and do things. This is important, it creates energy and it's powerful.
>
> Paul Adnitt: Former Head of Performance and Equalities The Learning Trust

> Our whole team is the same. We're very passionate about our subjects but we're also very passionate about doing as well as we can for the students in Hackney. We're part of the big picture so there's buy-in from teachers as well. It's not you and us, it's like we're in this together. It's led by my boss who has worked in Hackney for a number of years. Her children go to school in Hackney and there's a genuine belief that Hackney students can do as well as anyone else.
>
> Bukky Yusuf: Senior science consultant The Learning Trust

Increasing confidence is not about making people feel good. Feeling good about your work is an outcome of increased confidence, not the cause. We see in other

sections, particularly Challenge, how The Learning
Trust would not tolerate low standards. In driving
an organisation forward like this, there is a delicate
balance sometimes when confidence might be shaken
because the organisation's expectations are so high.
A deputy director is conscious of this.

> The high level of scrutiny, on balance, has been
> unhelpful because it could have made lots of
> people leave. Sometimes the scrutiny wasn't
> positive. At no point did anybody in the team we've
> got now say that it was good enough in primary,
> or that the outcomes were satisfactory. But we
> were quietly confident for the last few years that it
> was going to happen. I'm quietly confident about
> this year's national test results based on reliable
> information from our team. We hold ourselves to
> high account about the levels of improvement.
> We have high expectations. The minute we push
> past a boundary we go to the next one. Who cares
> about a floor target of 60%? We haven't let a SIP
> set a target of less that 65% for a few years.[68]
> We think level 4 is the minimum expectation, not
> the maximum.[69] We do well for our free school
> meal kids because they are the majority of our
> population.[70]

Tricia Okoruwa: Deputy Director The Learning Trust

We learn the combination of inspiration, building
relationships; challenge and support restored faith
and started to build confidence in Hackney. Kanter
discusses the importance of confidence in sustaining
winning streaks.[71] The Learning Trust soon fostered a
winning streak among schools in Hackney. A secondary
headteacher explains.

[68]Floor targets are set
by the Department for
Education. In 2011 the
floor target was that
60% of students in each
school should achieve
level 4 in English and
mathematics. Schools
which fail to meet
the floor target are
classified as under-
performing and they
are closely monitored.
A School Improvement
Partner (SIP) agrees
targets with a school for
performance in the next
year's tests.

[69]Level 4 is the expected
national curriculum
level for eleven year-
olds.

[70]Free school meals
are a welfare benefit
provided for children
from low income
families.

[71]Kanter, R.M. (2004)
Confidence. London:
Random House

> It's like that rolling snowball. Once it got out that Hackney was on this upward path, they wanted to join in. Success breeds success.
>
> Cheryl Day: Headteacher Clapton Girls' Technology College

The same headteacher reveals the friendly rivalry that exists between secondary schools in Hackney. This sustains confidence and drives things on.

> The first academy to produce GCSE results made the rest of us think 'We can do as good as that.' The only thing you can do is try to be as good as, if not better than them.
>
> Cheryl Day: Headteacher Clapton Girls' Technology College

We also find that confidence is sustained by celebration. The impact of this on students in schools is revealed by another secondary headteacher. Students are proud to attend schools in Hackney.

> The celebration of success is confidence building. I think the key about how you build success is to build confidence. It's about your self-esteem. The young people feel very confident about the way they look. When you walk around Hackney now, you'll see all the children in smart uniforms. They've got pride in their uniforms and in their schools.
>
> Jenny Wilkins: Principal Skinners' Academy

The re-furbishment of the existing secondary schools and the building of five new academies have raised confidence among parents. Secondary transfer has been reversed. Hackney schools are hugely over-subscribed with parents from other boroughs struggling to get their children into Hackney.

> Whatever your political views are on academies, there's no doubt that the building of five new schools in the borough has transformed the offer to parents. I've seen a huge difference at secondary transfer, now the majority of parents opt for a school in Hackney. The pattern of where children go at age 11 has changed dramatically. This year we have three children going out of the borough, out of 57. The reason these children are going is because their older siblings ended up in a school in another borough when the places were not available in Hackney. It's not just about academies because there are other schools in Hackney that are doing really well.

Karen Coulthard: Headteacher Berger Primary School

The principal of a new academy confirms parental demand for places in her school.

> In the first year we had 420 applicants for 118 places and all I could show parents was photographs of the building site. This year, after we moved in, we're up to 630 applicants. All the other academies will say the same.

Jenny Wilkins: Principal Skinners' Academy

We summarise the importance of building confidence through reflection by people in The Learning Trust. This was an important and deliberate strategy that was successfully implemented.

> I think taking education away from the Council seemed to make such good sense. I work with parents a lot and I see that they've got more confidence. We've got to put it down to parents who send their children to Hackney schools. They are the ones appealing to get their children into our schools. Why are they doing that? It's because

of the success. And it's not just about us here at The Learning Trust it's the parents who have confidence that their children will do well. There's competition now among parents to get children into our schools.

Lizzie Yauner: Head of inclusion team The Learning Trust

The Learning Trust stopped the madness and created an education service that people feel part of and proud of. Pupils, teachers, headteachers and governors all say what The Learning Trust did was to come in, get a hold of it and sort it out. We removed history and that baggage. We made it clear how important education is. We have created a platform where there are no excuses now, absolutely none. Nobody can blame the local authority, or teachers or poor recruitment. Nobody can blame the kids. We've shown that schools in Hackney can do as well as schools anywhere.

Alan Wood: Chief Executive The Learning Trust

I'm proud to feel that the people we put together as a team and the work of the Trust is widely recognised as having played a significant part in Hackney's rise. I feel very proud of that. I feel very proud that together we have improved the life chances of children, particularly working class kids who have had such a crap time in Hackney in the past decades. I think they were let down by education in this borough. To have played a part in the revival is extremely satisfying.

Alan Wood: Chief Executive The Learning Trust

Communication

Our lives begin to end the day we become silent about things that matter.
Martin Luther King Jnr

The Learning Trust realised from the beginning that it needed to establish good relationships with schools so that it could help them to improve. It wisely invested in a professional communications and marketing team and this investment paid off. Effective communication played a vital role is building relationships and helping to instil confidence in the workforce. The Learning Trust had ambitious proposals that relied on good partnerships with schools and others. We learn how the Trust initiated and maintained good communication so that these partnerships were fostered and confidence grew.

> I think The Learning Trust has been much better at listening to headteachers and asking them what they wanted.
>
> Lizzie Yauner: Head of inclusion team The Learning Trust

> He (Chief Executive) did quite a lot of talking with groups of heads, asking for our opinions on things. There was the start of a dialogue around us being users of services.
>
> Tricia Okoruwa: primary school headteacher at the time

The dialogue with secondary headteachers was crucial. In order to transform the secondary school provision, The Learning Trust needed to engage with the secondary school headteachers to reassure them and to avoid fragmentation. With only ten secondary schools at the time, it was easy to bring everyone together and develop the strategy that would lead to five new schools and massive refurbishments to the existing ones.

> There were meetings between all secondary
> heads, Mike Tomlinson and Alan Wood over a
> social event. Business was carried out over an
> evening meal. The secondary heads were engaged
> as a group quite quickly and collectively engaged
> as well. A lot of that was down to Mike Tomlinson
> who was highly respected. He never ever spoke to
> heads from the blame point of view. He set it up
> as a secondary working group and it has carried
> on all the way through, with academies and non-
> academies working together.

Tricia Okoruwa: Deputy Director The Learning Trust

With a larger number of primary schools it was not
possible to adopt the same approach. Nevertheless,
communication was improved as a primary
headteacher at the time remembers.

> I didn't feel as isolated as a head. I felt that there
> was better communication. There was more
> clarity about what the journey was that we were
> on. Somebody was articulating something at last.
> Mike Tomlinson played a significant role in that.
> I remember the first headteachers' conference
> when somebody actually said: 'These kids deserve
> something better and we're going to do it together.'
> It was much more purposeful.

Tricia Okoruwa: primary school headteacher at the time

Highly effective communication is a strong feature of
The Learning Trust today. It is succinctly explained by a
member of front line staff.

> I think that through communication is where
> a lot of the issues were solved. The ongoing
> communication about what was happening and
> what the expectations were, without criticism.
> It was communication; knowing where you're

going, knowing what the journey would be like. I think that was what helped people to focus in on it. When you had a target you had to change, you had to make a difference. Communication is always the key, whether it's Trust News coming out every week to update us or me coming to you if I've got a problem and discussing it with you. 🙶🙶

Ann Seago: Senior Family Information Officer The Learning Trust

We find excellent communications in all aspects of The Learning Trust's work. Communication was a high priority for Alan Wood as chief executive. Here is a governor talking about the school profiles.

🙶🙶 There is so much more information about each school that is shared now and it makes such a difference. A report comes out each year and puts every single school on the map and tells them where they sit in relation to other schools in the borough. When it first came out some headteachers were against it but now it's one of the best working documents going. It empowers governors to ask the right questions. 🙶🙶

Peter Passam: Governor of the Best Start Federation; the strategic management board of the federated PRU & non-executive director The Learning Trust

Honesty and integrity are essential for good communication. Sometimes this requires sensitivity when people are told things they would rather not hear about their performance or their school. Over time this develops trust on both sides as communication is a two-way process.

🙶🙶 There's a much more relaxed communication between the schools and The Learning Trust. I think that's built on trust and consistency of our word. It took a while to develop and it took a

while for teachers to understand that we weren't
Hackney Council anymore.

Neil Weeks: Corporate Governance Officer The Learning Trust

What makes The Learning Trust stand out from local
authorities is their communications and marketing
team. The Trust has invested wisely in this aspect of its
work. The communications team has made a significant
contribution to building confidence among students,
parents and teachers in Hackney.

The marketing work that was done is amazing.
You don't really see that in other education
departments. I think that was a master stroke.
To start to invest in that strand, to start building
aspirations through lots of strong visual imagery,
lots of campaigns in the press. Trailblazers played
a major part.

Paul Adnitt: Former Head of Performance and Equalities The
Learning Trust

There is no magic wand here though. It needs a
persistent approach over time to reach the community.

For parents and the community it took a good four
or five years into the contract for them to know and
understand that there was a significant difference
in what they were getting. I don't think it was
immediate. But I think one of the strengths of The
Learning Trust was that right from the beginning it
had a communications and marketing strategy to
change the image of Hackney schools. Any good
news we could get out there was got out there. The
schools started to buy into that as well and started
looking for opportunities. How we used the media
to re-create a different story from the history as it
was perceived was quite powerful.

Tricia Okoruwa: Deputy Director The Learning Trust

Effective communications have made a real difference
to the working conditions for staff in The Learning Trust.
They feel highly valued by the organisation and this in
turn is reflected in the services they provide.

> The Learning Trust morning conference, where we
> all come together, develops a corporate identity.
> You talk to different people at the conference and
> that helps things develop. We've got a choir in The
> Learning Trust, a football team, a netball team.
> That's brought a lot of well-being. The possibilities
> of working across services to support each other.
> Communication has been a million times better.
> The majority of people here feel quite nurtured.
> The value of that is having a group of people who
> feel nurtured going out to schools and wanting to
> nurture them.
>
> Lizzie Yauner: Head of inclusion team The Learning Trust

Celebration

Celebrate what you want to see more of.
Thomas J Peters

The decision to make celebration a high priority came from discussions with headteachers when The Learning Trust started. 'Teacher of the Year' awards are relatively new to the English education system; some people still find the idea of singling people out for praise a bit strange. In 2002, it was a brave new way of doing things in Hackney and it initiated a complete change in culture by 2011. The Chief Executive explains how he listened to heads and developed the strategy.

One group of the more thoughtful heads told us that even when Hackney schools do well no one takes any notice, no one celebrates our success. So part of the strategy was to celebrate success. We invested in the communications and marketing team. They introduced programmes like Trailblazers and The Learning Trust awards. We pushed lots of headteachers into the national teaching awards and supported them. We won all kinds of teaching awards, all sorts of awards for our work on recruitment and we won an award for getting Hackney reading.[72] By celebrating success right from the start I think we helped to create the culture that says 'You're doing really important things.'

Alan Wood: Chief Executive The Learning Trust

Although it was strange in the beginning, it soon caught on as Mike Tomlinson tells us.

We decided that we needed to celebrate good things that happen in Hackney. So we initiated two awards evenings: one for students and one for schools. It just happened that the first one was

[72]'Words Unite – Get Hackney Reading' was a community campaign to ensure all children could read by age 7.

for students and it coincided with the re-opening of the Hackney Empire. So we held it in the Hackney Empire. As this was a new idea, it wasn't particularly well attended. But five years later it was like trying to get tickets for the Olympics.

Sir Mike Tomlinson: first Chair of The Learning Trust

The awards were only one strand of an explicit and high-profile marketing campaign initiated by a dedicated communications and marketing team in The Learning Trust. A primary head is conscious of the marketing campaign and acknowledges the change in culture.

One thing Mike Tomlinson said loudly and clearly was: 'We're going to turn this around. It's a no blame culture and I'm out for good press'. He promoted Hackney schools and the good news got out there. Now, when you're out of school and you meet other colleagues and they ask where you're from and you say Hackney, you don't get the same negative reaction you got a few years ago. It's now an award culture and that feels different.

Karen Coulthard: Headteacher Berger Primary School

A secondary head agrees.

Before we were so busy with the drive to get on and doing things that we weren't sharing what we were doing. The Learning Trust started to bring in things like Trailblazers which was absolutely clear about this is our success. All the good news stories were gradually filtering through. Suddenly there were good news stories in the Hackney Gazette. You started to see our students' success in national newspapers.

Jenny Wilkins: Principal Skinners' Academy

It didn't happen overnight, it took time to develop. At first it was unusual to read or hear any good news about

Hackney schools in the local or national media. Good relationships were established with the press who were continuously fed stories about great things going on in Hackney. Journalists are always seeking good copy that they can quickly turn into news. The Learning Trust started to supply it, but let's not forget they needed something good to write about in the first place.

> " We've done a really good communications and marketing job about sharing the success of our secondary schools' results. And rightly so."
>
> Tricia Okoruwa: Deputy Director The Learning Trust

Estelle Morris reminds us that Hackney was front page news in the national press for the wrong reasons before The Learning Trust was established. After Government intervention she was relieved when Hackney no longer hit the headlines. Her relief is because this indicated that the intervention was turning things around.

> " I always knew Hackney was a success when it went out of the headlines. When two years passed and Hackney wasn't the story when the school performance tables came out, you almost breathed a sigh of relief. It's easy to forget how dire the situation was and how much we were letting down children. And while it has been a steady and sustained improvement, it really has been a revolution in a decade."
>
> Estelle Morris: Secretary of State for Education and Skills 2001–2002

We find the combined effect of the awards that signal appreciation and the consistent publication of good news about Hackney schools in the local press have created a huge confidence in Hackney which is shared by the community and the workforce in schools and in The Learning Trust. That confidence generates an upward spiral as people feel good about their work and

themselves which, in turn, ensures they continue to
grow and improve the services they provide. Somebody
who has worked on the frontline of Hackney education
services since 1971 speaks eloquently on behalf of
many people we listened to in The Learning Trust.

> For your passion to be my passion you need to
> feel you make a difference. We definitely feel we
> make a difference, we're encouraged to think that
> way and we're encouraged to think we can make
> an even bigger difference. Now the things that we
> have done are appreciated and that helps. I feel
> totally valued. I actually enjoy coming to work. I'm
> really positive about it and I think it has made a
> big difference. I'm just hoping that the difference
> carries on.

Ann Seago: Senior Family Information Officer The Learning Trust

It seems fitting that we should end this section
with a word of celebration from Estelle Morris, the
Government minister responsible for the intervention
and the establishment of The Learning Trust.

While Estelle deserves credit for initiating a remarkable
success story in terms of system-wide improvement
she acknowledges that the real work took place in The
Learning Trust and in Hackney schools.

> Politicians don't teach children and they don't lead
> schools, so they are constantly looking for levers
> for improvement. The idea of The Learning Trust
> was a brand new lever, it was a new vehicle. The
> people who gave life to it in Hackney really did
> gather the best around them and did a first-class
> job. It's been such a good news story that we are at
> risk of forgetting how it was done. It wouldn't have
> happened without The Learning Trust and they
> deserve huge credit for bringing it all about.

Estelle Morris: Secretary of State for Education and Skills
2001–2002

Consistency

There must be consistency in direction
W. Edwards Deming

Stable leadership in The Learning Trust ensured that policies were implemented and developed as time went on. This is an important condition for steady and sustained improvement in school test scores and GCSE results. The length of the contract was a critical factor to enable the Trust to develop a consistent way of working that would enable continued growth. Prospects are secure for continued improvement as long as things continue as they are. As the contract closes, there will always be a risk as the schools are transferred back to the Council. We learn how important safeguards have been established to ease this transition.

Time is a limiting factor for consistency. In order to prove its consistent support to schools, The Learning Trust needed time. A ten-year contract was considered appropriate in 2002; as the end of the contract approached, there were mixed views. People in the Trust would have preferred another few years so they could see more of their work reach fruition, while Hackney Council leaders felt the Council had proved itself reliable enough to administer education some years before.

> In prison education we went through this, where every five years we went out to tender again. I think five years is too soon. Probably eight years is a minimum but 10 years is a decent amount of time to make effective change.
>
> Tim Shields: Chief Executive Hackney Council

The improvements over the past ten years indicate that The Learning Trust needed and had sufficient time to develop a consistent and reliable service. While time may be a critical pre-requisite, on its own it does not necessarily lead to consistency. Here we learn about important features that enabled The Learning Trust to develop consistently high standards across Hackney.

Stable leadership would be no surprise. Alan Wood, who was appointed Director of Education by Hackney Council in 2001 and charged with the responsibility to lead the transfer of all education services in Hackney to The Learning Trust, has been the guiding light throughout. After serving as chief executive of The Learning Trust, he returned to Hackney Council in 2011 as Director of Children's Services to manage the transfer of education services back to the council at the end of The Learning Trust's contract. Alan's resolute leadership is a critical factor in this transformation and in 2011 he was awarded a CBE in recognition of his services to education and local government. Once appointed, all the senior leaders in the Trust have continued to work for the company since their recruitment in the first couple of years when the Trust was building its leadership team. Right from the outset, the chair and the chief executive were very explicit about their intentions:

> What they did was get into the trenches and said 'We're here to stay until we've solved this.' That made an immense difference.
>
> Richard Hardie: Chair of The Learning Trust

It's not just stable leadership, it runs right through the organisation. Once the right people have been recruited, they are developed and remain committed to their work. Professional growth and capacity building are also consistent.[73]

> We've had some key people who have been in place over the last five years. The school improvement team is now much more intellectual about their view of school improvement. When I compare the dialogue at the first meeting I went

[73] Capacity building is dealt with in its own section. See list of contents.

to as a primary adviser and the meeting I had last week for three hours when we were trying to unpick and pull together the leadership strategy and where we were going to go with it in the future, given the local authority's role is changing, it was a completely different quality of dialogue. 🙶

Tricia Okoruwa: Deputy Director The Learning Trust

🙶 They (schools) know who we are and there is confidence across The Learning Trust because we've all been here a very long time. I don't think any of the professionals in schools are worried about calling us to ask our opinion or to ask us what to do next. There's an atmosphere of trust. There's a confidence that they'll get 'How can we help?' There's much more of a 'You can do it yourself, but we're here to help you' attitude. We're not here to do it for them. 🙶

Lizzie Yauner: Head of inclusion team The Learning Trust

After leadership and growth, the next issue we find is the single focus on education. This point emerged frequently in our conversations and it makes sense. The Learning Trust had a very clear mission that we have already covered when describing the concept.

🙶 In The Learning Trust there is no political gain. Our work is solely with schools and education and our focus is clearly the outcomes. 🙶

Peter Passam: Governor of the Best Start Federation; the strategic management board of the federated PRU & non-executive director The Learning Trust

Without the involvement of elected politicians, whose priorities may not always be entirely on education, The Learning Trust has made unpopular decisions and acted on them swiftly. The political process, often characterised by lengthy periods of consultations and compromise, would hamper such concerted action.

> " The strength of The Learning Trust is that we haven't been subject to political whims or undue or unfair political influence. I think that has allowed us to make some quite tough decisions, particularly in the beginning around school closures. These were decisions that earlier would have been postponed or not dealt with as urgently. "

Neil Weeks: Corporate Governance Officer The Learning Trust

The single focus on education also meant that The Learning Trust's budget could not be diverted to other aspects of the Council's work as frequently happens in local authorities. Headteachers appreciate this because it enables them to develop more consistency in their schools through longer-term planning.

> " The resource and provision for children has been much more consistent over the last ten years. We haven't been prey to peaks and troughs or budget cuts and deficits. There's been a much more consistent approach to provision for children in Hackney no matter which school they happen to go to. That's had a huge motivational effect on staff. "

Sian Davies: Executive Principal Primary Advantage Federation

> " In terms of consistency, the funding hasn't been messed around. Some people have changed but there's enough who have stayed and that's helped. "

Cheryl Day: Headteacher Clapton Girls' Technology College

Stable leadership, professional growth, a single focus with a protected resource all contribute to a consistent approach and support for school improvement. This is essentially how The Learning Trust has helped schools in Hackney to achieve their current high standards.

> " There's been a very different think about what standards should look like and that's been generated by a more consistent approach from The Learning Trust as to what the standards and expectations mean. I don't think it's a question that it wasn't there before but I think now it's applied with rigour. Where schools are not meeting expectations there is a rapid response. People may feel differently about that but nevertheless there is a sense now that 'standards' is an issue that everyone shares and overall they are buying into. "

Karen Coulthard: Headteacher Berger Primary School

> " The upfront acknowledgement of what the schools are achieving and providing support for them without interference is a very tricky thing. That's what The Learning Trust has managed so skilfully, with stability and consistency. "

Cheryl Day: Headteacher Clapton Girls' Technology College

Not only is this clear for The Learning Trust, we find it is a strong feature of the highly successful primary federations.

> " A lot of the policies and systems we have are consistent across all five schools. It's the balance between prescription and autonomy that we have to strike very carefully so that we don't stop teachers being decision-making professionals in their own classrooms. We always try to strike the balance and that's an ongoing constant reminder. It's an important feature of our federation that we believe passionately in the individual nature of each school whilst drawing collectively from the shared practice and experience. "

Sian Davies: Executive Principal Primary Advantage Federation

As the end of the contract nears, the Chief Executive of Hackney Council is well aware that consistency is an important feature of the improvements that have been gained in the last ten years. In order to maintain this improvement, plans have already been put in place to ensure that leadership remains consistent.

> The relationships were built over a period of years. It was helped by the fact that we had stability with myself and Alan.
>
> The staff will be transferred across and we've ensured stability by making sure that Alan Wood who was the Chief Executive (of TLT) has now come (to the Council) as permanent Director of Children's Services. He is also in charge of the transition. So we've got that continuity. The key thing is to have a transition that doesn't affect school improvement. I don't see why it would apart from the fact that there are staff who are nervous about a change of organisation and perhaps a change of direction and ethos. That's a risk.

Tim Shields: Chief Executive Hackney Council

6 Conclusion

There is a growing body of evidence which shows conclusively how schools that serve high poverty communities can, and do, perform as well as any other schools. In many cases they outperform schools with a distinctly more privileged intake of students. In the 1990s, the National Commission on Education was funded by the Paul Hamlyn Foundation to investigate the reasons for under- achievement in deprived areas. Their report published in 1993 argued that in areas of multiple disadvantages the dice are loaded against educational success.[74] It was an argument for extra funding in these areas so that additional support could be provided which would improve the educational opportunities for children born in poverty.

Such an appeal can only be sustained by evidence which demonstrates how schools that serve children from disadvantaged backgrounds can succeed. In 1996 they published a book called 'Success against the odds' which was a collection of 11 individual case stories of highly effective schools in England, Northern Ireland, Scotland and Wales that serve disadvantaged communities.[75] This book was a major breakthrough at the time. Here was conclusive evidence that children from deprived backgrounds could perform as well as anyone else. While the study used a widespread sample of schools throughout the UK and the schools shone as beacons of hope, many of the schools were isolated examples of good practice. In all cases, there was a school just down the road serving a similar community where the children did not have the same quality of education.

[74] National Commission on Education (1993) Learning to Succeed. London: Heinemann

[75] National Commission on Education (1996) Success Against the Odds: Effective schools in disadvantaged areas. London: Heinemann

Since the introduction of regular Ofsted inspections of all schools in England in 1993, we now have a huge evidence base that reveals a complete picture throughout the country. Spend a few hours searching through the Ofsted website and you'll find many examples of outstanding schools serving disadvantaged communities with a failing school on their doorstep. Of course it may be argued that the oustanding school is part of the failing school's problem because it attracts the best students. We don't accept excuses like that. The issue is the impact of deprivation is more widespread than a single school. Research into school effectiveness and improvement is helpful but the units are wrong. In order to tackle disadvantage more systematically we need to look at high-performing education systems in deprived areas rather than individual schools. The story of how The Learning Trust transformed education in Hackney, one of the most severely deprived boroughs in England, is important in this context.

There is a similar situation in the United States. Barr and Parrett completed a meta-analysis of 18 research studies into high-performing high-poverty schools across the United States.[76] These studies were carried out between 1993 and 2005 and between them refer to hundreds of schools across 41 States. As in England, these studies were about schools rather than systems. One of the studies they refer to is 'Dispelling the Myth' by The Education Trust.[77] This is ongoing research over time and each year The Education Trust publishes case studies of high-performing high-poverty schools. Although the majority of cases are individual schools, the Education Trust has also reported about a few school systems, such as Massachusetts.[78]

Our study of how The Learning Trust transformed education in Hackney within ten years fills an important gap in three respects:

[76] Barr, R. & Parrett, W. (2007) *The Kids Left Behind: Catching up the under-achieving children of poverty* Bloomington: Solution Tree

[77] Education Trust (2002) D*ispelling the Myth ... over Time*. Washington: Education Trust

[78] Chenowith, K. (2009) *How It's Being Done: Urgent lessons from unexpected schools*. Cambridge: Harvard Education Press

1. It considers how an education system was improved, rather than individual schools.

2. The system was initially failing to provide an acceptable standard of education; subsequent improvements were swift and significant.

3. The system serves the most deprived community in London and is among the six most deprived boroughs in England.

   Our conclusion carries four important messages of hope for systemic improvement in deprived districts.

1. Create a powerful collective identity, or concept, that is built on actions rather than words. Everyone talks about moral purpose these days; consequently you need to demonstrate what you mean so you may be judged by your actions. If you are resolute and true to your word then you will inspire others to make similar commitments. Above all, maintain your integrity by being consistent.

2. Invest your energy and resources in capacity-building, you are guaranteed to show a profit. Our analysis of how The Learning Trust increased capacity across Hackney reveals four keys that build capacity:

a. Apply pressure by making high demands that will challenge schools to do better, no matter how well they may be doing.

b. Be brave and relentless, you will need courage to stick to your principles so don't expect an easy ride.

c. Take risks and be creative, innovation will be essential because whatever you were doing before didn't work.

d. Work together and support each other; collaboration creates synergy.

3. Never under-estimate the importance of confidence because everything depends on it. Confidence is the bridge between investment and results. Having made your wise investments, pay attention to confidence building. We learn from The Learning Trust how to boost confidence through effective communication and celebration.

4. It is time to think again about the link between poverty and under-achievement. We know there is a high correlation between poverty and low educational achievement. We have referred to substantial evidence through this study that shows conclusively that children from low-income families, schools that serve deprived communities and the education systems that support them can, and do, perform as well as anyone else. In our view it's time to ditch the contextual value-added measures that provide smokescreens to conceal inadequate teaching, leadership and support for schools. These measures are based on the assumption that poverty is the cause and low achievement the effect. We have referred to sufficient evidence to challenge this assumption. We believe it is more likely that low-achievement causes poverty. As educators it is time we got to grips with this and stopped using poverty as an excuse for under-achievement. Our most vulnerable children and young people deserve something better. The good news is that The Learning Trust and others show us how to do it.

7 Milestones

The Learning Trust has published a list of major achievements in each year of its existence. Need to update for 2011.

2002

- The Learning Trust is launched – the first not-for-profit private company to run educational services for an entire borough
- Hackney's Safer Schools Partnership is launched for all Hackney secondary schools
- 31 per cent of students achieve 5 or more GCSEs at A*–C

2003

- Chair of The Learning Trust Sir Mike Tomlinson publishes a major report into the future of 14–19 education
- 39 per cent of students achieve 5 or more GCSEs at A*–C

2004

- Mossbourne Community Academy opens
- Hackney's £167m Building Schools for the Future (BSF) programme is announced
- 45 per cent of students achieve 5 or more GCSEs at A*–C

2005

- The Hackney school students' Trailblazer programme is launched to recognise young people who have broken barriers and achieved excellence Yesoday Hatorah becomes Hackney's first Orthodox Jewish school to join the maintained sector

- Springfield Primary School opens

- 47 per cent of students achieve 5 or more GCSEs at A*–C

2006

- Petchey Academy opens

- 14 integrated children's centres are approved, offering education, health and social services under one roof for children and their parents

- 50 per cent of students achieve 5 or more GCSEs at A*–C

2007

- Bridge Academy opens

- Hackney students are among the first in the country to choose Diplomas

- The Learning Trust is awarded the national matrix quality kitemark for Education Advice and Guidance

- Words Unite, a community-wide campaign is launched to Get Hackney Reading. The year- long project led by The Learning Trust and funded by Team Hackney aims to encourage adults, children and young people throughout the borough to become enthusiastic, independent and inquiring readers.

- 54 per cent of students achieve 5 or more GCSEs at A*–C

2008

- More than 4,000 children perform in the 11th annual Hackney Schools Music Festival

- A £2.6m Play Pathfinder scheme is launched to provide new adventure playgrounds and exciting and innovative play areas for children and young people in the borough

- 56 per cent of students achieve 5 or more GCSEs at A*–C

2009

- City Academy opens
- Hackney's GCSE results pass above the national average for the first time
- More than 1,500 pupils take part in the largest inclusive sports schools events in the country
- 67 per cent of students achieve 5 or more GCSEs at A*–C

2010

- Hackney's 14–19 results make it the most improved in the country at Key Stage 4 and the second most improved (per student) at Post-16
- BSF work completed at Stoke Newington School and Clapton Girls' Technology College
- Skinners' Academy opens
- All-new Berger Primary School opens
- 71 per cent of students achieve 5 or more GCSEs at A*–C

2011

- 75 per cent of students achieve 5 or more GCSEs at A*–C

8 Conversation

We recorded conversations with the following people:

Paul Adnitt, Former Head of Performance and Equalities TLT

Donna Anthony, Senior Primary Admissions Officer TLT

Steve Belk, Director of Learning and Standards TLT

Ophelia Carter, Head of Schools Finance TLT

Karen Coulthard, Headteacher Berger Primary School

Sian Davies, Executive Principal Primary Advantage Federation

Cheryl Day, Headteacher Clapton Girls' Technology College

Anthony Greenidge, Inclusion Officer TLT

Richard Hardie, Chair of The Learning Trust Board & non-executive director

Liz Hutchinson, Corporate Communications Manager TLT

Caroline King, Headteacher Colvestone Primary School

Marion Lavelle, Head of Admissions TLT

Leroy Logan, Non-executive director The Learning Trust

Michael McCabe, Governor Services Officer TLT

Estelle Morris, Secretary of State for Education & Skills 2002

Michael O'Reagan, Head of Corporate Governance TLT

Tricia Okoruwa, Deputy Director Primary Education TLT

Peter Passam, Governor of the Best Start Federation; the strategic management board of the federated PRU & non-executive director The Learning Trust

Elaine Peers, Head of Partnerships & Safeguarding TLT, former Head of School Place Planning TLT

Heather Rockhold, Former Headteacher Lauriston Primary School & non-executive director The Learning Trust

Diane Roome, Former Headteacher Gayhurst Primary School

Ann Seago, Senior Family Information Officer TLT

Valerie Serrette Figaro, Headteacher Randall Cremer School

Yvonne Servante, Deputy Director Secondary Education TLT

Bill Sheasgreen, Governor Stoke Newington School

Tim Shields, Chief Executive Hackney Council

Trish Smith, Head of Adult Learning TLT

Laurel Theodosiou, School Attendance Officer TLT

Sir Mike Tomlinson, Former Chair of The Learning Trust

Mike Vance, Caribbean Achievement Co –ordinator TLT

Neil Weeks, Corporate Governance Officer TLT

Jenny Wilkins, Principal Skinners' Academy

Alan Wood, Chief Executive Learning Trust & Director Children's Services for Hackney

Lizzie Yauner, Head of Inclusion Team TLT

Harriet Young, Head of Admissions and Pupil Benefits TLT

Bukky Yusuf, Senior Science Consultant TLT

References

Audit Commission (2000). Hackney LBC Corporate Governance Inspection

Barr, R. & Parrett, W. (2007). *The Kids Left Behind: Catching up the underachieving children of poverty*. Bloomington: Solution Tree

Barber, M. (1996). *The Learning Game*. London: Victor Gollancz

Barber, M. (2009). From System Effectiveness to System Improvement: Reform Paradigms and Relationships in Hargreaves, A. & Fullan, M. (eds) *Change Wars*. Bloomington: Solution Tree

Barber, M. & Mourshed, M. (2007). *How the World's best-performing school systems come out on top*. New York: McKinsey & Co.

Barker, P. (2000). Hackney Council a load of rubbish in *London Evening Standard* 9 November

Boyle, A. (2007). Compassionate Intervention in Blankstein, A., Cole, R. & Houston, P. (eds) *Engaging Every Learner*. Thousand Oaks: Corwin

Cassidy, S. (2001). Hackney council stripped of right to run schools in *Independent on Sunday* 18 October

Chenowith, K. (2009). *How it's being done: Urgent lessons from unexpected schools*. Cambridge MA: Harvard Education Press

Communities and Local Government (2011). *The English Indices of Deprivation 2010*. London: HMSO

Department for Education and Science (1990). *Schools in Hackney: Some Issues. A Report by HMI*. London: Department for Education and Science

Education Trust (2002). *Dispelling the Myth...Over Time*. Washington: Education Trust

Farson, R. (2007). The Case for Failure in Blankstein, A., Cole, R. & Houston, P. (eds) *Engaging Every Learner*. Thousand Oaks: Corwin

Fink, D. (2005). *Leadership for Mortals*. London: Paul Chapman

Fullan, M. (2008). *Six Secrets of Change*. San Francisco: Jossey-Bass

Fullan, M. (2010). *All Systems Go*. Thousand Oaks: Corwin

Hansard (1997). *House of Commons Official Report Parliamentary debates*. 1 December columns 130–132

Hargreaves, A. & Fink, D. (2006). *Sustainable Leadership.* San Francisco: Jossey Bass

Hargreaves, A. & Shirley, D. (2009). *The Fourth Way: The inspiring future for educational change* Thousand Oaks: Corwin

Hargreaves, A. et al (2011). P*erformance Beyond Expectation*. Nottingham: National College for School Leadership

Kanter, R.M. (2004). *Confidence*. London: Random House

Leithwood, K., Janzi, D. & Steinbach, R. (2000). *Changing Leadership for Changing Times*. Milton Keynes: Open University Press

Maclean, D. (2001). Challenge and support to schools in Woods, D. & Cribb, M. (eds) *Effective LEAs and School Improvement*. London: Routledge Falmer

Mourshed, M., Chijioke, C. & Barber, M. (2010). *How the World's most improved school systems keep getting better.* New York: McKinsey & Co.

National Commission on Education (1993). *Learning to succeed.* London: Heinemann

National Commission on Education (1996). S*uccess Against the Odds: Effective schools in disadvantaged areas*. London: Heinemann

Office for Standards in Education (1999). *Lessons learned from special measures*. London: Ofsted

Office for Standards in Education (2000). *Inspection of Hackney Local Education Authority*

Raffo, C. et al (2007). *Education and Poverty: Mapping the terrain and making links to educational policy.* Manchester: Joseph Rowntree Foundation

Walker, D. & Smithers, R. (1999) Borough of hate and hit squads in *The Guardian* 19 March

Whitehead, M. (1994). Labour set to bar the party within, in *Times Educational Supplement* 9 August

Index

10cc 20–21, **23**

A
Academies programme 43–48, 83, 90–91, 95–97, 110
Adnitt, Paul 76, 84, 105, 107, 115
Audit Commission 12, 13

B
Barber, Sir Michael 2
Barr, Robert 128
Belk, Steve 41, 48, 51, 54–55, 82, 97
Berger Primary 133
Blair, Tony PM 2, 31
Blunkett, David 11
Boyle, Alan 3
Building Schools for the Future 43 90, 131, 133
Byers, Stephen 11

C
capacity 23, **53**
celebration 28, **117**
challenge 24, **66**
Change Wars 2
City Academy 133
Clapton Girls' Technology College 133
closing schools 82
Closing the gap 15–18, **19**
collaboration 26, 61, **93**
communication 28, **112**
communications & marketing team 115
competition 71–72
concept 23, **30**
confidence 27, **102**

consistency 29, **121**
contract length 121
Coulthard, Karen 64, 71, 110
courage 25, **76**
creativity 25, **84**

D

Davies, Sian 69, 72, 75, 78, 86, 99–100, 124, 125
Day, Cheryl 47, 59, 75, 90, 104–105, 106, 109, 124, 125

E

Elliston, Tony 1
executive principal 99
external consultants 55

F

federations 61–63, 97–100, 125
ferocious assertion 66
find & fix 49–50
Fink, Dean 29
floor targets 108

G

GCSE results 8, 10, 13, 15–16, 131–133

H

Hackney Action Research Project 9
Hackney borough 7
Hackney Council 10, 12, 29, 33, 43–44, 52, 93–94
Hackney Downs 10, 46
Hackney household survey 8
Hackney Improvement Team 2, 11
Hardie, Richard 39, 41, 66, 69, 76, 85, 86, 91, 95, 96
Hargreaves, Andy 3, 4
HMI 9
Holy Trinity Primary 98
Humphreys, Salli 3

I

ILEA 4, 8
international collaboration 63
intervention 68–69, 78

J

John, Gus 9, 10

K

Kingsland school 81
Kingsmead Primary School 10
KS2 national test results 17–18

L

Langham, Lorraine 1
leadership programme 57–58
Learning Trust structure 34–35

M

McCabe, Michael 71
McKinsey & Co 3
Morris, Estelle 6, 30–36, 119–120
Mossbourne Academy 46, 131

N

National Commission on Education 127
national strategy 87
NCSL 57–58
Nord Anglia 11, 12, 33, 53

O

Ofsted 10, 12, 13, 50
Okoruwa, Tricia 38–39, 41, 49–51, 56, 60, 63–64,
        68, 73, 74, 77–78, 80, 87–88, 92, 97–98, 100,
        102–103, 112–113, 115, 119, 122–123

P

Parrett, William 128
Passam, Peter 45, 51, 59, 61–62, 74, 86, 105, 106, 114,
        123
Peers, Elaine 42, 44, 46, 70, 96
Performance Beyond Expectations 3–4
Petchey Academy 132
poverty & achievement 128–130
predict & prevent 49–50
professional development centre 89
Puttnam, Lord 29

R

Reid, Liz 11, 12
research method p4–5
risk-taking 91

S

Seago, Ann 40, 72–73, 113–114, 120
secondary strategy 67–68
Sedgemoor, Brian MP 1
self-esteem 102
Shields, Tim 34, 40, 46, 52, 94, 121, 126
single focus 124
Skinners' Academy 133
St John & St James Primary 98
stable leadership 122
Stoke Newington School 56, 133
Success against the odds 127

T

teaching quality 74
Tomlinson, Sir Mike 13, 30, 36–38, 42, 44–45, 48, 57,
        81, 85, 89, 95, 103, 104, 106, 117–118, 131
Trailblazer programme 131
transition 126

W

Weeks, Neil 54–55, 103, 114–115, 124
Wilkins, Jenny 37, 80, 83, 109
Williams, Shirley Baroness 28
Wood, Alan 13, 39–40, 43, 65, 67, 69, 79, 81, 85, 89, 106, 111, 117, 122
Woodhead, Chris 33
Words Unite 88, 117, 132

Y
Yauner, Lizzie 50, 70, 104, 110–111, **112**, 116, 123
Yusuf, Bukky 58, 87–88, 101, 107